T0243606

MILITARY DRONES

MILITARY DRONES
UNMANNED AERIAL VEHICLES (UAVs)

ALEXANDER STILWELL

amber
BOOKS

First published in 2023

Published by Amber Books Ltd
United House
London N7 9DP
United Kingdom
www.amberbooks.co.uk
Facebook: amberbooks
Instagram: amberbooksltd
Twitter: @amberbooks
Pinterest: amberbooksltd

ISBN: 978-1-83886-291-6

Editor: Michael Spilling
Designer: Mark Batley
Picture research: Terry Forshaw

Printed in China

CONTENTS

INTRODUCTION

Military drones, or unmanned aerial vehicles (UAVs), are one of the fastest-growing new technologies in modern warfare. Although it would not be possible to provide a comprehensive account of such a proliferating growth area, this book covers significant unmanned aerial vehicles (UAVs), unmanned combat aerial vehicles (UCAVs) and vertical take-off and landing (VTOL) UAVs in service or development around the world. Legacy UAVs in various sizes and forms pioneered many of the technologies and capabilities that are so familiar today. Intelligence, surveillance and reconnaissance (ISR) UAVs are one of the largest areas of drone use and development. These 'eyes in the sky' provide a wealth of information to both strategic commanders, as well as frontline soldiers and special forces. Unmanned combat aerial vehicles (UCAVs) are perhaps the fastest-growing and most technically

PROTECTOR RG MK 1 (MQ-9B)
A British-operated Protector drone undergoes tests at RAF Waddington, UK.

advanced area of drone technology. These drones enable commanders to not only identify threats, but also to carry out surgical strikes when necessary. Vertical take-off and landing (VTOL) UAVs are covered both in conventional helicopter form, as well as hybrids that can lift and land vertically and also transition into conventional fixed-wing flight. UAVs and UCAVs in development are also discussed, including the exciting advances in teaming between manned aircraft and 'loyal wingman' UCAVs, which provide vital force-multipliers for the air forces of tomorrow. Such is the exponential and fast-paced growth of drone technology that it is clear tomorrow is not far away.

Technological advances

The rapid development of unmanned aerial vehicles since the 1980s – when their tactical value, first spotted by Israel, was more widely appreciated, not least by the United States – went hand in hand with developments in technology, including the microprocessor and more efficient video technology. In both cases, miniaturization

and cost-effectiveness meant that complex tasks could be handled by compact instruments that could be fitted into a relatively small aerial vehicle. Video compression and digitization meant that high-quality imagery could be relayed live to an operator on the ground and immediately assessed by intelligence personnel. Improvements in global positioning system (GPS) technology from the late 1970s onwards enabled unmanned aerial vehicles to be flown on pre-programmed routes and return to base. Satellite up-links resolved the problem of radio links being interrupted by atmospherics, terrain or enemy jamming, which meant that unmanned aerial vehicles could be successfully controlled over the horizon. Camera technology continued to be developed in the civil and military markets, cross-loading the benefits of research and keeping costs down. The proliferation of drone technology meant that smaller companies became involved in defence contracts, although sometimes they were acquired by larger defence companies who appreciated their technical expertise.

Engine developments

All the components that make up an unmanned aerial vehicle have seen developments, including UAV engines.

EAGLE B-HUNTER
A B-Hunter UAV is operated from a Belgian army control room.

Both large and small UAVs require engines that are both fuel-efficient for long-endurance missions as well as having a low acoustic signature. This is vital, for example, for a special forces unit sending up a small reconnaissance drone in a covert environment, whether in a forest or urban area. Established companies such as Rolls-Royce and Rotax are joined by companies focused on renewable energy such as SkyPower. Whether two-stroke or four-stroke, engines also have to be compatible with military grade fuels. To maximize efficiency, range and endurance, stealth technologies have continued to be developed, including flying-wing designs capable of hypersonic speeds. Projects such as BAE Systems/University of Manchester's MAGMA have even dispensed with traditional moving surfaces in the quest to minimize friction.

From hand-launched, backpackable small UAVs to airpower teaming systems in support of advanced fighter jets, this book aims to provide a thorough overview of one of the most rapidly developing phenomena of current and future aerial warfare.

LEGACY UNMANNED AERIAL VEHICLES

The legacy unmanned aerial vehicles listed in this chapter represent the UAVs that in many ways pushed back the boundaries and demonstrated, sometimes in combat, what a UAV could do.

The story of the development of UAVs is often one of high aspirations broken against the wall of bureaucracy and technical limitations. However, there is nothing like an emergency to concentrate the mind and to make things work from whatever resources are available.

RQ-2 PIONEER
An RQ-2 Pioneer operated by the US Marine Corps 3rd RPV platoon returning from a mission during Operation Desert Shield during the 1991 Gulf War. The Pioneer was also deployed by the US Navy and the US Army.

9

War in Lebanon

During the crisis in the Middle East in the 1980s, Israeli Aircraft Industries (IAI) and Tadiran both developed viable UAVs in the form of the Scout and Mastiff respectively that would prove their worth during the War in Lebanon (1982–85). The Scout and Mastiff played a key role in identifying and monitoring Syrian surface-to-air missile (SAM) batteries in the Bekaa Valley that were limiting the ability of the Israeli Air Force (IAF) to provide aerial cover for the Israeli Defense Forces (IDF). The Israelis mounted a sophisticated electronic warfare campaign that included flying Mastiff drones over the Libyan missile batteries so that the Syrian radars locked on to the UAVs. The signals were then transmitted by the Mastiffs back to Scout UAVs flying in a stand-off position. They, in turn, relayed the signals to Grumman EC-2 Hawkeye aircraft flying offshore that provided co-ordinates for Phantom F-4 jets to fire missiles at the SAM batteries.

Deploying Scout and Mastiff

When the Syrian air force responded by sending in their

IAF PHANTOM

An Israeli Air Force (IAF) Phantom jet fighter flies over the Lebanese capital of Beirut, August 1982.

MiG-21 and MiG-23 fighters, the Scout and Mastiff UAVs were deployed to assess how many Syrian aircraft had taken off. EC-2 Hawkeye aircraft then guided Israeli Air Force F-15 Eagle and F-16 fighter aircraft towards the oncoming Syrian fighter jets and in such a way as to maximize the vulnerability of the Syrian jets to side-on attacks. The Israeli fighters were armed with Sparrow and Sidewinder missiles that almost invariably defeated the MiG fighter defences. It was one of the most significant air battles since World War II and the overmatch of Western technology versus Soviet technology sent shockwaves through the Kremlin.

However, the air superiority of the F-15 Eagles was largely owed in this case to the reconnaissance work of the humble Israeli-designed Scout and Mastiff UAVs.

This lesson was not lost on the United States, which decided to short-circuit its UAV programme by acquiring a Scout-inspired UAV. Israeli Aircraft Industries (IAI) worked with AAI Corporation to develop the Pioneer UAV, which would prove to be a mainstay of the US Army, US Navy and US Marine Corps for years to come.

As the communist bloc began to break up, leading to a host of new security challenges not least in the Balkans, there was increased demand for UAVs to monitor borders without the potential political inconvenience of manned aircraft being shot down. In the United States, it was decided to circumvent the bureaucracy of long-winded acquisition programmes through the Department of Defense and instead route the UAV

"The well-named Pioneer was a groundbreaking unmanned aerial vehicle first developed for the US Navy…"

acquisition through the CIA. This led to the development of the General Atomics/Leading Systems Gnat, which in turn led to the development of the Predator.

RQ-2 Pioneer

The well-named Pioneer was a groundbreaking unmanned aerial vehicle first developed for the US Navy, which then became a valued asset for both the US Marine Corps and the US Army. US Military operations in the 1980s, including Canada, Lebanon and Libya, highlighted a need for a straightforward unmanned aerial vehicle that could provide over-the-horizon targeting, reconnaissance and battle damage assessment (BDA) for local commanders. Initially, in 1986, the Pioneer was deployed on the recommissioned Iowa-class battleship USS *Wisconsin*.

MQ-1 PREDATOR
An armed MQ-1 Predator
deployed by the 15th
Expeditionary Reconnaissance
Squadron as part of Operation
Iraqi Freedom, Ali Al Salem
Airbase, Kuwait.

Radar
The bulbous area at the
front of the UAV houses
essential payloads, including
radar and a satellite
communications system.

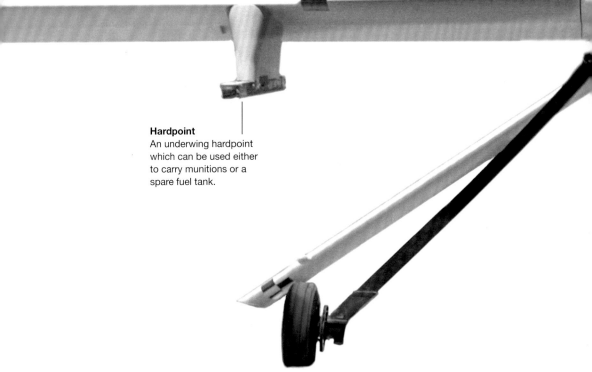

Hardpoint
An underwing hardpoint
which can be used either
to carry munitions or a
spare fuel tank.

Gimbal
The gimbal incorporates an AN/AAS-S2 multi-spectral targeting system, a colour nose camera, a variable aperture day TV camera and a thermographic camera.

Munitions
This Predator is armed with AGM-114 Hellfire missiles for precision strikes.

RQ-2 PIONEER SPECIFICATIONS

Weight:

118.69kg (416lb)

Dimensions:

L: 4m (13.1ft); Wingspan: 5.20m

(17.1ft); H: 1.1m (3.3ft)

Powerplant:

Sachs SF-350 petrol engine

Range/Endurance:

185km/h (100nmi)

Service ceiling:

4.5m (15,000ft)

Speed:

165km/h (124mph)

Weapons:

N/A

The Pioneer proved ideal for gunnery spotting duties. The following year, the US Marine Corps began fielding the Pioneer and by 1990 the US Army was also operating the UAV.

Valuable asset in Iraq

It was to be a valuable asset for all three branches of the services during the ensuing conflict against Iraq after the invasion of Kuwait in 1991. This would prove to be an ideal theatre in which the Pioneer could demonstrate its qualities. The Pioneer flew in over 300 missions during the conflict, including a successful interception of Iraqi fast patrol boats that were threatening the US fleet. There were also various mishaps and losses of aircraft, including losses as a result of enemy action and

RQ-2 PIONEER

An RQ-2B Pioneer unmanned aerial vehicle is attached to the pneumatic launch truck before takeoff at Al Taqaddum, Iraq. The Pioneer is used for basic reconnaissance with a variety of missions ranging from collecting data for battle damage assessments to calling in air support as a forward observer.

RQ-2 PIONEER

Country of origin:
United States

Manufacturer:
AAI Corporation

Operators:
US Navy; US Marine Corps;
US Army

First flight: 1986

Don't Shoot

First launched in 1943, the Iowa-class battleships USS *Missouri* and USS *Wisconsin* had been designed for war with Imperial Japan and specifically to compete with fast Japanese battleships of the era. Their designers would not have envisaged the ships being involved in a high-tech conflict about half a century later. Having been decommissioned after the end of World War II, both ships were recommissioned and modernized in the late 1980s, including the addition of Tomahawk cruise missiles alongside their original batteries of formidable 406mm (16in) guns. USS *Wisconsin* also received eight RQ-2 Pioneer UAVs to provide artillery spotting and battle damage assessment. After the invasion of Kuwait by Iraq in 1991, both battleships were deployed to the Gulf and were some of the first into action. On 23 February, USS *Missouri* was firing on Iraqi positions on Faylaka island offshore from Kuwait City. As USS *Wisconsin* approached to relieve her sister ship, she deployed an RQ-2 Pioneer towards the island. The UAV was flown deliberately at a low altitude to indicate to the Iraqi defenders that there would soon be more 406mm (16in) shells on the way. As the Pioneer approached the Iraqi positions, the soldiers started waving white flags and other white materials to indicate their surrender. This was passed on to the captain of USS *Wisconsin* by the UAV controllers onboard. It was the first time in the history of warfare that soldiers had surrendered to an unmanned aerial vehicle.

RQ-2A PIONEER
Pioneer RQ-2A UAV (A20000794000) at the Smithsonian Institution National Air and Space Museum. This was the exact drone deployed by USS *Wisconsin* on 23 February 1991.

GNAT-750 SPECIFICATIONS

Weight: 254kg (560lb)

Dimensions: L: 5m (16ft 5in);
Wingspan 10.77m (35ft 4in)

Powerplant:
Rotax 912 piston engine

Range/Endurance:
48 hours

Service ceiling:
7620m (25,000ft)

Speed:
193km/h (120mph)

Weapons: N/A

crashes. While the 'money men' complained about the mounting costs, military commanders were far more positive. As far as they were concerned, the Pioneer had proved its worth and a lost UAV was far less expensive than the loss of a full-size manned reconnaissance aircraft; and more importantly did not result in the loss of any American lives. The Pioneer features a pusher propeller, twin tail booms and rudder, and straight wings, made from fibreglass braced with balsa wood. The fuselage is made from aluminium as are the wing spars, tail booms and landing-gear struts. The Pioneer can be launched with an on-board rocket, which is then jettisoned, or it can be launched from a catapult. Recovery is either by a net system or an arrester wire picked up by a tailing hook. The Pioneer can be broken down into its constituent parts

and packed into a container. The aircraft can be controlled by two operators from a ground control station (GCS) or flown autonomously with an autopilot programmed to follow a certain flight path. The aircraft can also be controlled from a portable control system (PCS) that enabled soldiers on the ground to take control of the aircraft. A remote receiving station (RRS) provided a video display with real-time imagery for commanders on the ground. The Pioneer is fitted with a gimbal-mounted electro-optical/infrared (EO/IR) sensor that can relay analogue video in real time with a line-of-sight data link.

Gnat-750

The Gnat-750 was a development of a project by Leading Systems called Amber. Leading Systems was bought by General Atomics and the project continued to

be developed as the Gnat-750 Tier 1. At this stage, the Gnat was not fitted with a satellite uplink antenna and therefore the UAV relied upon an RG-8 powered glider to relay signals back to the ground station. The Gnat-750 was equipped with a forward-looking infrared system (FLIR) and both daylight and low-light TV cameras. It could also be fitted with a GPS navigation system for fully autonomous missions. The Gnat-750 was powered by a Rotax 912 piston engine and featured straight wings on an extended fuselage with a sloped nose. The tailplanes were angled downwards.

The Gnat-750 was significant in the development of the post-Vietnam US UAV programme and it was a vital stepping stone to the UAVs still flying today. Acquired through the CIA in order to circumvent US Department of Defense bureaucracy, the Gnat-750 was deployed to former Yugoslavia to monitor peacekeeping operations. Here it demonstrated both its potential and its limitations. Lessons learned led to the production of an improved Gnat, the I-Gnat, which featured a turbocharged engine and other modifications that gave it better reliability and performance.

Further improvements led to the creation of a version with a satellite uplink called the Predator.

GNAT-750

Country of origin:
United States
Manufacturer:
General Atomics Aeronautical Systems
Operators:
Central Intelligence Agency (CIA)
First flight:
1989

RQ-14 DRAGON EYE
A US Marine launches a Dragon Eye UAV for reconnaissance of a supply road. The Dragon Eye UAV could be easily carried in a backpack and could be deployed by a single soldier to provide squad-level reconnaissance.

RQ-14 DRAGON EYE SPECIFICATIONS

Weight:
4.7kg (5.9lb)

Dimensions:
L: 0.91m (3ft); Wingspan: 1.14m (5.75ft)

Powerplant:
Electric motor

Range/Endurance:
5km (3.1mi)

Service ceiling:
91–152m (300¬500ft)

Speed:
64km/h (40mph)

Weapons:
N/A

RQ-14 DRAGON EYE

Country of origin:
United States

Manufacturer:
AeroVironment

Operators:
US Marine Corps

First flight:
2001

RQ-14 Dragon Eye

The Dragon Eye was a small reconnaissance unmanned aerial vehicle (UAV) that was developed by the Naval Research Laboratory and Marine Corps Warfighting Laboratory and manufactured by AeroVironment. Its purpose was to provide essential eye-in-the-sky battlefield assessment in a miniature package that could be easily handled by a single soldier. Lightweight and easy to assemble, the Dragon Eye could be carried in a backpack and launched by hand. Once airborne, the Dragon Eye used its waypoint-based navigation system, which could be pre-programmed by the operator. This worked with an integrated Global Positioning System (GPS) and inertial navigation system.

The Dragon Eye has rectangular wings with a propeller located under each wing. It has no tailplanes and no undercarriage. The air vehicle is designed to break up in a safe way if it should crash to preserve intact the electronic equipment onboard. The air vehicle is controlled from a rugged laptop computer.

The RQ-14 Dragon Eye was deployed by the US Marine Corps during the 2003 invasion of Iraq but in due course it was replaced by the more sophisticated RQ-11 Raven B.

FQM-151 Pointer

Developed on behalf of the US Army, US Marine Corps and Naval Special Warfare, the FQM-151 Pointer was a small unmanned aerial vehicle designed for battlefield surveillance. Manufactured from high-impact Kevlar, the

FQM-151 POINTER

Country of origin:
United States
Manufacturer:
AeroVironment
Operators:
US Army; US Marine Corps; US Navy
Special Operations Command
First flight:
1988

Pointer was a fixed-wing air vehicle with wings sitting on a pylon above the fuselage and an electric engine and pusher propeller located behind the wing. The Pointer carried a CCD camera in the nose and, as its name suggests, the air vehicle needed to be pointing directly at the area of interest to collect relevant imagery. This was relayed to the operator via a radio or fibre-optic link and was recorded on a video cassette from which it could be replayed at various speeds. The air vehicle and the control station could be carried in two separate backpacks.

The Pointer system was deployed by both the US Army and Marine Corps during Operation Desert Storm in 1991 and it was also used by US Navy SEAL Team 3 operators at the beginning of Operation Iraqi Freedom in 2003. It was proven in trials that the Pointer could be successfully launched from the deck of a submarine. In due course, the Pointer was replaced by the AeroVironment RQ-11 Raven and RQ-20

FQM-151 POINTER SPECIFICATIONS

Weight:
4kg (9lb)
Dimensions:
L: 1.83m (6ft); Wingspan: 2.74m (9ft)
Powerplant:
Electric motor
Range/Endurance:
1 hour
Service ceiling:
300m (1000ft)
Speed:
73km/h (46mph)
Weapons: N/A

FQM-151 POINTER

United States Navy Special Warfare Combatant-Craft Crewmen launch an FQM-151 Pointer UAV during a Black Sea patrol in 2019.

Special Forces Strike Missions

Special forces have always been at the forefront of the development of new technology and have consistently demanded the highest standards from the systems that they use. The US Navy SEALs have used small UAVs such as the Pointer from the early days of development for find, fix and strike missions and for other purposes. These systems were in due course replaced by more sophisticated UAVs that fulfilled the demanding mission requirements of the SEALs. The Pointer proved its worth when it was used by SEAL Team 3 during Operation Iraqi Freedom in 2003. It was replaced in due course by UAVs such as the Raven, Puma and ScanEagle, which are discussed in Chapter 2. The Navy SEALs also developed a doctrine for use of UAVs, including direct action (DA) operations, special reconnaissance (SR), counterterrorism (CT) and foreign internal defence (FID).

Puma. Arguably, the Pointer was an important stage in the development of these two successful UAVs. In 2022, the US Army placed yet another order for the RQ-20 Puma.

RQ-5 Hunter

The RQ-5 Hunter played an important role in the development of unmanned aerial vehicles and it was one of the first UAVs to be employed in active operations with the US Army. First introduced in 1996, the Hunter was a large unmanned aerial vehicle that featured twin engines at each end of the fuselage, with one propeller pulling and the other pushing. It had fixed main wings and twin tails on the end of extended booms. The MQ-5B version featured advanced avionics as well as hard points under the wings to carry munitions. The electronics package included an integrated Global Positioning System (GPS), forward-looking infrared

(FLIR), a laser designator, VHF/UHF communications and electronic countermeasures.

The Hunter system consisted of three ground control stations (GCS), six Hunter aerial vehicles and six EO/IR day/night packs. The Hunter system was designed to provide real-time imagery intelligence, artillery forward observation, battle damage assessment, reconnaissance and surveillance, target acquisition and battlefield observation. Hunters had the capability of operating in pairs whereby two airborne aircraft would relay communications over a C-band line-of-sight data link.

Deployments

Hunter systems were deployed to Macedonia and Kosovo in 1999 in support of Operation Allied Force. Although one Hunter was shot down by Yugoslav forces, the system proved its worth in the mountainous terrain of the

Balkans. In 2003, Hunters were deployed in support of Operation Iraqi Freedom where they flew over 600 reconnaissance, surveillance and target acquisition missions. Hunters were also deployed by the Belgian armed forces in 2006 in support of the European Union Force (EUFOR) in the Congo.

In 2007, a Hunter operated by US forces in Iraq dropped a laser-guided munition. This was the first armed mission by an unmanned aerial vehicle flown by the US Army. Hunter systems were also deployed in Afghanistan where the system provided valuable intelligence in the rugged terrain.

Although an extended version of the Hunter with double the wingspan was developed, by then US armed forces were looking at other systems such as the RQ-1C Gray Eagle. There was, however, no doubt about the groundbreaking contribution

MQ-5B HUNTER

Country of origin:
Israel/United States
Manufacturer:
Northrop Grumman
Operators:
US Army; Belgian armed forces;
French armed forces
First flight:
1996

that the Hunter had made
or of its contribution to an
understanding of the value of
unmanned aerial systems and
their potential for the future.

Tadiran Mastiff
The Tadiran Mastiff was one
of the most significant modern
military drones and, along
with the IAI Malat Scout, it
played a significant role in
the development of drone
technology and tactics. The
Tadiran had a simple and robust

design, including a rectangular
fuselage that housed the
necessary avionics and mission
equipment, a pusher propeller
at the back of the fuselage and
twin vertical tailplanes on the
end of two booms. It carried
a video camera and had the
ability to send high-resolution
video imagery to its operators.
Three variants of the Mastiff
were produced.

IAI Malat Scout
The Scout was developed in
the 1970s and was regularly
used by the Israeli Defense
Forces (IDF) and the Israeli Air
Force (IAF) in various combat
roles. It was deployed in the
1982 Lebanon war to identify
Syrian surface-to-air missile
sites. During their deployment
to Lebanon in 1983, US military
forces took an interest in the
Scout and its capabilities
and in due course a joint
US–Israeli project led to the

RQ-5A HUNTER
The RQ-5 Hunter was a successful early
reconnaissance UAV which was deployed
to Macedonia to support NATO forces
in Kosovo. The Pointer was operated on
a relay basis, with two UAVs airborne
simultaneously.

MQ-5B HUNTER SPECIFICATIONS

Weight:
725kg (1600lb)
Dimensions:
L: 7.1m (23ft); Wingspan: 8.84m
(29ft); H 1.7m (5.6ft)
Powerplant:
Twin Mercedes HFE Diesel
3-cylinder engines
Range/Endurance:
260km (162mi)
Service ceiling:
4,572m (15,000ft)
Speed:
204km/h (127mph)
Weapons:
GBU 44/B 'Viper Strike' munitions

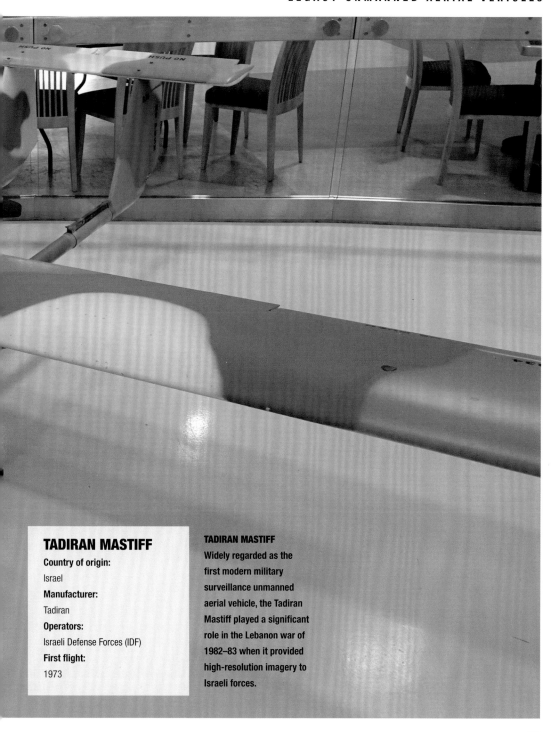

TADIRAN MASTIFF

Country of origin:

Israel

Manufacturer:

Tadiran

Operators:

Israeli Defense Forces (IDF)

First flight:

1973

TADIRAN MASTIFF

Widely regarded as the
first modern military
surveillance unmanned
aerial vehicle, the Tadiran
Mastiff played a significant
role in the Lebanon war of
1982–83 when it provided
high-resolution imagery to
Israeli forces.

development of the Pioneer, which was deployed by the US Army and Marine Corps. The design of the Scout, including a pusher propeller at the rear of the fuselage and twin-boom tailplanes, was a template for future UAVs such as the Searcher.

IAI MALAT SCOUT

Along with the Tadiran Mastiff, the Scout played a significant role in establishing the reconnaissance UAV as an essential tool on the modern battlefield.

IAI MALAT SCOUT SPECIFICATIONS

Weight:

96kg (211lb)

Dimensions:

L: 3.68m (12ft 1in); Wingspan: 4.96m (16ft 3in)

Powerplant:

16KW piston engine

Range/Endurance:

7 hours 30 minutes

Service ceiling:

4600m (15,000ft)

Speed:

176km/h (109mph)

Weapons: N/A

IAI MALAT SCOUT

Country of origin:

Israel

Manufacturer:

IAI Malat

Operators:

Israel Defense Forces (IDF)

First flight:

1970s

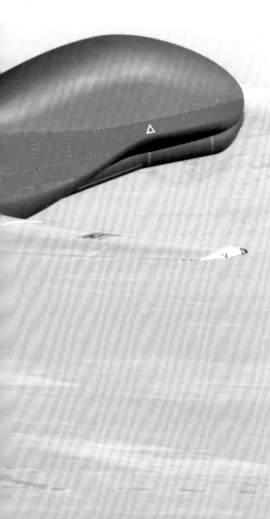

INTELLIGENCE, SURVEILLANCE & RECONNAISSANCE

From the earliest days of warfare to the present, military reconnaissance has been a vital tool for field commanders and strategists. The more you know about your enemy's positions, movements, strength, equipment and armaments the easier it is to make informed decisions. Perhaps the most effective early use of aerial reconnaissance was during World War I when commanders were eager to obtain details of enemy dispositions on an otherwise flat and static battlefield. Forward observation officers (FOOs) had a dangerous life as they were priority targets for enemy snipers and it was difficult for them to gain the height they needed to gain useful information. Aerial reconnaissance, therefore, provided a good opportunity to map the battlefield and spot potential targets. Aircraft such as the Bleriot XI, Moraine-Saulnier Scout and Farman MFII from the French Aeronautique Militaire; German Aviatik, Rumpter and Taube aircraft; and the Avro 504, BE2 and RE8 flown by the British Royal Flying Corps were fitted with downward-pointing cameras. The British developed the Watson air camera, which provided overlapping photography. When the United States entered the war they contributed new technology such as the tri-lens camera. So far as military commanders at the time were concerned, aerial reconnaissance was much more important than the limited advantages gained in aerial dogfights.

RQ-4A GLOBAL HAWK

An aerial view of the maiden flight of the second US Navy RQ-4A Global Hawk UAV en route to Edwards Air Force Base, California, June 2005.

EARLY RECONNAISSANCE
This modified Graflex camera was used for aerial reconnaissance during World War I. Aerial reconnaissance proved to be vital to intelligence officers during the war both for battle planning and damage assessment.

During World War II, aerial reconnaissance continued to provide vital information. The Royal Air Force Photographic Reconnaissance Development Unit operated fast aircraft such as the Supermarine Spitfire PR.XIX and de Havilland Mosquito. During this period there were improvements and adaptations to aircraft and equipment to maximize the chances of the reconnaissance aircraft surviving the mission and returning to base with its valuable film. As they often flew over highly protected areas, speed was essential and the Spitfires of the PRU were often stripped of all unnecessary

equipment including armaments and radios to reduce weight and increase speed. The aircraft were fitted with downward-looking F-4 cameras, either in the wings or the fuselage.

Cold War
During the Cold War, the superpowers wanted to gain as much information about each other and their allies as they could. The United States flew U-2 aircraft over the Soviet Union but as surface-to-air SA missiles developed, the flights became more perilous. After a U-2 was shot down on 1 May 1960, research into unmanned

alternatives was accelerated. One of these was the D-21 Tagboard, which was capable of flying at speeds of over Mach 3. The D-21 UAVs were designed to be expendable and to drop their camera pods before they crashed. There were some mishaps in which the aircraft failed to release the pod or the UAV was shot down. The Soviet Union developed a long-range reconnaissance drone called the Tupolev TU-123 Yastreb with an autonomous flight system. This could fly at Mach 2 at 19,800m (65,000ft). Like the US D-21, the drone was designed to eject its camera before crashing.

Vietnam

During the Vietnam War, the United States operated small UAVs called Ryan 147 Lightning Bugs. These were developed over time to include versions that could operate by night, a signals intelligence (SIGINT) variant and one with a capability for jamming enemy radar. Apart from North Vietnam, Lightning Bugs were also flown over China and

> ## "The Soviet Union developed a long-range reconnaissance drone called the Tupolev TU-123 Yastreb with an autonomous flight system."

North Korea. The Vietnam War proved to be the largest deployment of reconnaissance in a combat environment up to that time.

Middle East

Israel began to experiment with UAVs during the 1973 Yom Kippur War against Egypt and Syria. By the early 1980s, Israeli companies Tadiran and Israeli Aircraft Industries (IAI) had developed the Mastiff and Scout UAVs to provide

LOCKHEED D-2A

This 1960s supersonic reconnaissance drone was deployed from either an M-21 reconnaissance aircraft or a Boeing B-52 Stratofortress. It was used during the Cold War but suffered several mishaps before the programme was terminated in 1971.

RYAN MODEL 147

Known as the Lightning Bug, this remotely piloted vehicle (RPV) was produced in several variants to carry out aerial reconnaissance, surveillance and signals intelligence missions mainly during the Vietnam War between 1982 and 1975.

real-time surveillance using available and inexpensive video technology. These were two of the most significant modern reconnaissance and surveillance unmanned aerial vehicles. During the 1982–85 Lebanon War, the Mastiff and Scout UAVs made a vital contribution to identifying Syrian surface-to-air (SA) missile batteries, allowing

Israeli Air Force (IAF) F-15 Eagle and F-16 fighter aircraft to demonstrate their superiority over Syrian MiG-21 and MiG-23 fighters. Unmanned aerial reconnaissance had reached a watershed moment and proven its worth.

NATO

One of the most successful reconnaissance UAVs deployed

by NATO forces from the 1960s through to the 1990s was the Canadian CL-289 Midge. This UAV had the appearance of a missile and transitioned from jet power at launch to turbojet for the pre-programmed mission. On return, parachutes would slow the vehicle and slow its descent to the ground, upon which airbags were inflated to cushion the landing. In the United States and the United Kingdom, programmes such as the Aquila and the Phoenix failed to get off the ground. The United States was so impressed with the IAI Scout that it promoted the development of a joint project between IAI and AAI, which produced the Pioneer UAV. The Pioneer was deployed successfully in both the 1991 Gulf War and the 2003 invasion of Iraq.

War on Terror
After the 11 September 2001 attacks in the United States, UAV systems were rapidly deployed over Afghanistan, including the Predator and the Global Hawk, although the latter was still in pre-production testing. As the campaigns in Afghanistan and later Iraq developed, there was increased use of handheld backpackable small UAVs that could be easily assembled and launched either by hand, by catapult or from moving vehicles. UAVs such as the Desert Hawk or RQ-11 Raven, which had been developed for US Special Operations Command (USSOCOM) could provide real-time reconnaissance for small units in order to circumvent ambushes and to spot IEDs.

Syria
The Syrian civil war began in 2011 and continues in 2022. The major Russian intervention in the war was between 2015 and 2016 and during this

CL-289
A CL-289 drone is launched by French forces in Bosnia and Herzegovina in November 1986. Developed by Canadair, this reconnaissance and surveillance drone was deployed by Canada, the United Kingdom, West Germany, France and Italy.

RQ-11 RAVEN SPECIFICATIONS

Weight:

2.1kg (4.8lb)

Dimensions:

L: 0.9m (3 ft); Wingspan:

1.37m (4ft 5in)

Powerplant:

Direct driven electric motor

Range/Endurance:

10km (6.2mi)

Service ceiling:

46–152m (150–1,000ft)

Speed:

41.8km/h (26mph)

Weapons:

N/A

period they deployed over 1700 UAVs. Defence analysts have suggested that Russia used the Syrian conflict to refine the integration of UAVs into its order of battle.

The Russian drone fleet was largely focused on intelligence, surveillance and reconnaissance (ISR), producing accurate targeting information for Russian artillery, multiple-launch rocket systems (MLRS) and strike aircraft. Russian commanders were provided with real-time information around the clock, which enhanced their decision-making process.

Conflict in Nagorno-Karabakh

This conflict began in 1988 when ethnic Armenians demanded the transfer of the Nagorno-Karabakh autonomous oblast from Soviet Azerbaijan to Armenia, and tensions exploded into a war that ended in 1998. However, it was the short war between September and November 2020 that was most significant so far as the use of UAVs is concerned. Although Armenia used the Russian-made Orlan-10 reconnaissance UAV to good effect, Azerbaijan fielded a much wider spectrum

of UAVs that helped it to dominate the skies and the battlefield. These included the Hermes 900, Hermes 450, Heron, Aerostar and Searcher reconnaissance UAVs. They also used armed drones, which are discussed in more detail in Chapter 3. The use of these UAVs gave Azerbaijan a significant advantage in intelligence, surveillance and reconnaissance (ISR) in addition to long-range strike. The UAVs were tied into a network that included both aerial strikes by manned aircraft as well as artillery. Their precise targeting contributed to the neutralization of large numbers of Armenian mobile and static assets, including tanks and air defences. As the air defences were degraded so was their ability to counter UAV strikes. This conflict was an early warning to the world that the side that managed their UAV assets better would have the advantage.

War in Ukraine

During the early stages of the war in Ukraine in 2022, Russia deployed predominantly reconnaissance UAVs for artillery spotting and targeting whereas Ukraine deployed large numbers of unmanned combat aerial vehicles (UCAVs), such as the Bayraktar TB2, which are discussed

ABOVE: DRONE TRAINING
Ukrainian servicemen train using commercial drones in a military capacity to spot and target enemies for artillery teams in Kharkiv Oblast, Ukraine on August 2022.

OPPOSITE: RQ-11 RAVEN
A Raven reconnaissance UAV is launched by a soldier in Afghanistan in 2011. The Raven is a highly portable UAV deployed by US Special Operations Command and provides essential reconnaissance for small fighting units.

MQ-1C GRAY EAGLE
An MQ-1C Gray Eagle of 10th Aviation Regiment prepares to deploy from Al Asad Air Base, Iraq, September 2017.

MQ-1C GRAY EAGLE SPECIFICATIONS

Weight:
N/A

Dimensions:
H 2.1m (6ft 11in); Wingspan: 17m (28ft)

Powerplant:
Lycoming IDEL-120 Heavy Fuel Engine (HFE)

Range/Endurance:
37.4km (230mi) / 25 hours

Service ceiling:
8,839m (29,000ft)

Speed:
309km/h (192mph)

Weapons:
AGM-114 Hellfire or AIM-92 Stinger

in Chapter 3. Russian intelligence, reconnaissance and surveillance (ISR) UAVs, such as the Orlan-10, greatly reduced the time between target identification and an artillery fire mission. Whereas conventional spotting methods would take between 20 and 30 minutes between identification and firing, the UAVs cut this down to about five minutes. Due to the effectiveness of intelligence, surveillance and reconnaissance UAVs, it is no surprise that both sides made a high priority of either jamming UAVs or shooting them down. As the war continued and more and more specifically military drones were lost, both sides and Ukraine in particular started to replace their expensive purpose-built advanced technology military UAVs with adapted commercial models, thus significantly

reducing costs. Due to the comparatively limited resources on the Ukrainian side, including artillery shells, the UAVs were an effective means of making each shot count, rather than expending large numbers of shells in a barrage that might or might not hit the target. To counter this, the Russian side used radar jamming against Ukrainian military UAVs and electronic measures against commercial UAVs in order to disrupt their signals. This battle between the UAVs, including the measures used to counter them, would help to shape warfare of the future.

General Atomics MQ-1C Gray Eagle
Developed by General Atomics as an upgrade of the MQ-1 Predator for the US Army, the MQ-1C Gray Eagle was designed to provide increased

MQ-1C GRAY EAGLE

Country of origin:
United States
Manufacturer:
General Atomics Aeronautical Systems
Operators:
US Army; US Special Forces
First flight:
2004

range, altitude and payload over previous systems. The Gray Eagle's design brief covered a variety of challenging service requirements that included persistent reconnaissance, surveillance and target acquisition (RSTA) as well as attack operations. Although early versions of the Gray Eagle exhibited reliability issues, these were addressed by the manufacturers and in July 2013 an improved Grey Eagle was launched. The new

model featured improved fuel and payload capacity as well as a modified Lycoming IDEL-120 Heavy Fuel Engine (HFE). The engine is designed to run on either jet fuel or diesel to support the US Army's "single fuel in the battlefield" concept. The Gray Eagle is also fitted with an automatic take-off and landing system.

The Improved Gray Eagle (IGE) made enough of an impression for the US Army to order it for its intelligence and special forces groups. Deliveries were made to 160th Special Operations Aviation Regiment (Airborne) (160th SOAR) with a target of 12 aircraft each for two SOAR companies. Each package of 12 aircraft is accompanied by a support system that includes six universal ground control systems; nine ground data terminals; 12 mobile ground control stations; one ground

data terminal; Light Mobile Tactical Vehicles (LMTVs) and other ground-support assets operated and maintained by a company of 105 soldiers.

In June 2022, it was reported that the US Government were considering the sale of four MQ-1C medium-altitude long-endurance (MALE) drones to Ukraine. This would give extra offensive ability to the Ukrainian forces, but would also require considerable training for operators to manage this sophisticated system.

Northrop Grumman RQ-4C/RQ-4B Global Hawk

This unmanned, high-altitude, long-endurance aerial reconnaissance system was developed by Northrop Grumman in partnership with Ryan Aerospace in the late 1990s. In 2001, it received

RQ-4 GLOBAL HAWK
This illustration shows the Rolls-Royce-North American F137-RR-100 turbofan engine, Satellite communications system and payloads that include active electronically scanned array radar and electro-optic/infrared sensors.

RQ-4 GLOBAL HAWK SPECIFICATIONS

Weight:

6781 kg (14,950lb)

Dimensions:

L: 4.5m (4ft 6in); Wingspan:
39.8m (130ft 9in)

Powerplant:

Rolls-Royce North American
F137-PR-100 turbofan engine

Range/Endurance:

22,780km/h (12,300 nmi)

Service ceiling:

18,288m (60,000ft)

Speed:

574km/h (357mph)

Weapons:

N/A

RQ-4C / RQ-4B GLOBAL HAWK

Country of origin:

United States

Manufacturer:

Northrop Grumman

Operators:

US Air Force; US Navy; NATO

First flight:

1998

a contract from the US Department of Defense for low-rate initial production. The terror attacks on New York and Washington on 11 September 2001 brought forward the deployment of Global Hawk before full testing had been completed, and it played a significant role in the wars in Afghanistan and Iraq. However, the loss of several aircraft due to technical failures led to the development of an improved version of Global Hawk, designated RQ-4B. Apart from various technical modifications and improvements it also featured a larger nose section and wider wingspan. The US Air Force aircraft were deployed by US Air Combat Command and its various reconnaissance squadrons.

RQ-4N and MQ-4C Triton

The US Navy also took an interest in the programme and an RQ-4N version was produced to meet the US Navy's Broad Area Maritime Surveillance (BAMS) requirement. The package included active electronically scanned array (AESA) radar. The naval version also featured strengthened wing structures due to the naval requirement for the aircraft to descend rapidly to lower altitudes to carry out closer focused mission requirements.

US Air Force: 'Global Hawk's mission is to provide a spectrum of ISR collection capability to support joint combatant forces in worldwide peacetime, contingency and wartime operations.'

Apart from its primary military mission of identifying potential threats in order to enable commanders to make informed decisions, Global Hawk can also provide vital information for civil authorities to predict threatening weather conditions or monitor natural disasters. NATO ordered a version of Global Hawk,

MQ-4C TRITON

An MQ-4C Triton unmanned aerial vehicle approaches landing at Naval Air Station Patuxent River. The MQ-4C Triton is designed for maritime operations and has the ability to carry out reconnaissance at lower altitudes than the US Air Force Global Hawk.

designated the RQ-4D Phoenix, as part of its Alliance Ground Surveillance (AGS) programme. Individual countries such as Germany and Australia also considered the aircraft. The German version was developed in collaboration with the European Aeronautic Defence and Space Company to carry a signals intelligence (SIGINT) package but the programme ran into certification issues with regard to German airspace and the programme was shelved. The Royal Australian Air Force has ordered the MQ-4C version. South Korea ordered four Global Hawk RQ-4B aircraft and Japan plans

SCANEAGLE SPECIFICATIONS

Weight:

18kg (9.7lb)

Dimensions:

L: 1.19m (3ft 9in); Wingspan: 3.1m (10ft 2in)

Powerplant:

3W 2-stroke piston engine

Range/Endurance:

18 hours

Service ceiling:

5,950m (19,500ft)

Speed:

148km/h (92mph)

Weapons:

N/A

LAUNCH CATAPULT

A ScanEagle operated by the US Marine Corps stands ready to be launched from its 'Super Wedge' catapult launch system.

to purchase three aircraft, the first of which was delivered in March 2022.

Boeing Insitu ScanEagle

The ScanEagle is a small unmanned aircraft system (UAS) with capabilities that include intelligence, surveillance and reconnaissance (ISR). With its long endurance, the ScanEagle can provide surveillance of areas of interest to the commander with minimal risk of being observed or intercepted. It is capable of flying at an altitude of 4572m (15,000ft) over a 24-hour mission, making it a valuable asset for mission planning and target verification.

SCANEAGLE

Country of origin:
United States
Manufacturer:
Boeing Insitu
Operators:
US Air Force Special Operations Command; US Marine Corps; Royal Australian Navy; Royal Navy; Canadian Defence Force
First flight: 2002

At 1.19m (3.9ft) in length and with a wingspan of 3.1m (10.2ft), the ScanEagle is powered by a heavy fuel (JP-5 or JP-8) engine. The ScanEagle system consists of four air vehicles (AVs), a ground control station, a remote video

Captain Phillips hostage incident

In April 2009, the cargo ship *Maersk Alabama*, a Danish-owned ship with a US crew under the command of Captain Richard Phillips, was en route from Salalah, Oman, bound for Mombasa, Kenya, via Djibouti. There had been several pirate incidents in these waters and the *Maersk Alabama* was sailing alone. On 9 April, the ship was approached by two skiffs carrying pirates from Somalia. One of the pirate skiffs managed to evade the countermeasures used by the ship, including flares and fire hoses, and the pirates boarded the ship. Some of the crew locked themselves in a strong room but Captain Phillips was held by the pirates. Realizing that they would not be able to control the ship, which had been closed down, the pirates escaped in a closed lifeboat but took Captain Phillips with them as a hostage, hoping to ransom him once they reached the mainland.

The US Navy deployed the guided missile destroyer USS *Bainbridge* and the guided missile frigate USS *Halyburton* to the area. USS *Bainbridge* carried a ScanEagle system onboard, which it deployed to search for the lifeboat. A Boeing Global Services and Support Intelligence, Surveillance and Reconnaissance (ISR) team aboard USS *Bainbridge* successfully located the lifeboat in the Indian Ocean with the ScanEagle, which used its sensors to send electro-optical and infrared still and video feeds back to the warship, enabling US Navy warships to intercept.

Daring SEAL rescue

Once the warships came close to the lifeboat, naval and FBI negotiators tried to broker a deal for the release of Captain Phillips. Meanwhile, US Navy SEAL snipers of Red Squadron Naval Special Warfare Development Group parachuted into the sea near USS *Halyburton* and were then transferred to USS *Bainbridge*. As talks with the pirates broke down and tension mounted, the snipers took up positions on the fantail of USS *Bainbridge* and selected their targets. When it was clear that the life of Captain Phillips was in danger, the snipers adjusted their aim against the roll of the ship and of the lifeboat and squeezed their triggers. Three pirates on board the lifeboat were killed and Captain Phillips was rescued unharmed. In this extraordinary operation, which demanded the highest levels of professionalism, the ScanEagle provided vital reconnaissance and surveillance that enabled the US Navy to rescue Captain Phillips.

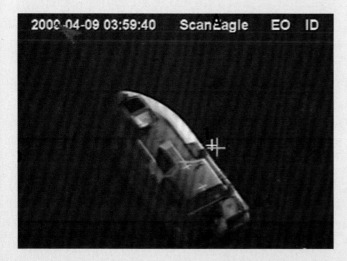

DRONE'S EYE VIEW
A still taken from real-time imagery obtained by a ScanEagle UAV of the life raft commandeered by Somali pirates from MV *Maersk Alabama* and in which Captain Phillips was held hostage. Reconnaissance from the ScanEagle enabled US navy ships to intercept the craft before US Navy SEALs intervened and Captain Philipps was rescued.

RQ-21A BLACKJACK SPECIFICATIONS

Weight:

61.2kg (135lb)

Dimensions:

L: 2.5m (8ft 2in); Wingspan:

4.7m (15ft 7in)

Powerplant:

8 HP reciprocating engine

with EFI (JP5/JP-8)

Range/Endurance:

16 hours

Service ceiling:

6,090m (20,000ft)

Speed:

111km/h (69mph)

Weapons:

N/A

RQ-21A BLACKJACK

An RQ-21A Blackjack unmanned
aerial surveillance aircraft, attached
to Marine Medium Tiltrotor Squadron
365 (Reinforced), in flight after being
launched from the flight deck of the
amphibious transport dock ship USS
Mesa Verde (LPD 19), April 2017.

RQ-21A BLACKJACK

Country of origin:

United States

Manufacturer:

Boeing Insitu

Operators:

US Navy; US Marine Corps

First flight:

2012

terminal, a 'SuperWedge' launch system and a Skyhook recovery system. The ScanEagle can be launched either from land or from a ship and it is retrieved by a cable tethering system controlled by differential GPS. The UAS carries a stabilized electro-optical and/or infrared camera in an inertial stabilized turret that is fitted with INSTAR NanoSTAR synthetic aperture radar. In service with US Air Force Special Operations Command, US Marine Corps, Royal Navy, Royal Australian Navy and Canadian Defence Force among others, the ScanEagle has been deployed in a variety of contingency and combat operations worldwide. These include deployment to Iraq in 2004 and in Operation United Protector during the Libyan revolution of 2011.

RQ-12A WASP III

An infantryman of 2nd Infantry Division launches a Wasp III by hand, demonstrating how easy it is to deploy. The Wasp III is also used by Special Operations Forces for essential area reconnaissance.

Boeing Insitu RQ-21A Blackjack (Integrator)

This small tactical unarmed system (STUAS) was built to meet a requirement by the United States Navy. Designed to complement and supplement the ScanEagle, the twin-boom RQ-21A uses the same launcher and recovery system.

The RQ-21A Blackjack can provide long-duration day and night intelligence, surveillance and reconnaissance (ISR) in an economically packaged craft. Despite its modest size, the RQ-21A is capable of delivering vital information in real time for commanders. Like the ScanEagle, the Blackjack can be deployed from either land or from ships. With its open-architecture design, the Blackjack can be adapted to carry a variety of payloads according to mission requirements. These may include an infrared tracker, laser range finder, daylight full-motion video, a communications relay package, synthetic aperture radar/ground moving target indicator (SAR/GMTI) and signals intelligence. It is modular, flexible and multi-mission capable.

The RQ-21A is delivered as a system that includes five air vehicles, two ground control systems and launch and recovery support equipment. It has been deployed by the US Marine Corps' Unmanned Aerial Vehicle (UAV) Squadron (VMU) 2 and 3. The US Navy employ the system for special operations, among other tasks such as anti-piracy operations and search and rescue (SAR).

AeroVironment RQ-12A Wasp IV

The Wasp RQ-12A small unmanned aircraft system (SUAS) was developed by AeroVironment and the Defense Advanced Research Projects Agency (DARPA) for US Air Force Special Operations Command (AFSOC). The AFSOC requirement was for a beyond-line-of-sight situational awareness asset for use by US Air Force Special Operations Command Battlefield Airmen. The package came under the AFSOC Battlefield Air Targeting Micro Air Vehicle (BATMAV) programme.

The Wasp is a lightweight micro air vehicle equipped with a two-bladed propeller driven by a small electric motor. It carries an inertial navigation system and an auto-pilot as well as two infrared cameras with forward and side-viewing capability. The aircraft can be programmed to either fly autonomously from take-off to landing or be controlled manually by a ground controller. The Wasp system consists of an air vehicle, ground control unit and a communications ground station. The whole system can be carried by a special forces operator in a backpack.

The revised Wasp AE (RQ-12A) has greater endurance than the original version and also has the ability to operate over land and on water. This version was selected by the US Marine Corps.

RQ-11 Raven

The RQ-11 Raven is one of the most successful and widely deployed small unmanned aircraft systems (SUAs). It is deployed by various branches of the US armed forces as well as armed forces worldwide. In the US armed forces, the Raven is part of the Small Unit Remote Scouting System (SURS). It provides beyond-line-of-sight intelligence to company and smaller units. It was deployed by the US Air Force under its Force Protection Airborne Surveillance System (FPASS)

RQ-11 RAVEN

A US military policeman from 89th Military Police Brigade launches a Raven UAV during an exercise in Germany, 2018.

RQ-11 RAVEN SPECIFICATIONS

Weight:
2.1kg (4.8lb)
Dimensions:
L: 0.9m (3 ft); Wingspan: 1.37m (4ft 5in)
Powerplant:
Direct driven electric motor
Range/Endurance:
10km (6.2mi)
Service ceiling:
46–152m (150–1,000ft)
Speed:
41.8km/h (26mph)
Weapons:
N/A

programme. It is also in service with the US Marine Corps and US Special Operations.

The Raven is capable of providing intelligence, surveillance, target acquisition and reconnaissance day or night. The gimbal camera in more recent versions of the Raven can switch between day and night sensor modes.

The RQ-11 Raven is supplied as a system that includes three air vehicles, a ground control station (GCS), a remote video terminal, a gimbaled electro-optical/infrared (EO/IR) camera, a field repair kit, batteries and spares.

The Raven can be set to fully autonomous mode, which includes navigation, altitude hold, loiter and return modes. All this can be viewed and selected by the controller from a rugged laptop that includes Portable Flight Planning Software/Falcon View Planning Software. Raven has a wide range of use, including force protection and convoy security, and it is also a useful asset for military operations in urban terrain (MOUT).

The Raven is the most widely used small unmanned aircraft system among military forces worldwide. It was used by UK forces in Iraq and by Danish forces in Afghanistan. It is also in use with the Dutch army, marine corps and special forces. The United States supplied Raven systems to Ukraine during its struggle against the Russian invasion.

AeroVironment RQ-20 Puma

The Puma is a small unmanned aircraft system (SUAS) primarily designed for intelligence, surveillance, reconnaissance and targeting (ISRT). It was acquired by US Special Operations Command (USSOCOM) under its All Environment Capable Variant (AECV) programme and was later deployed more broadly by the US Army, US Marine Corps, US Air Force and various military forces worldwide. The aircraft is fully waterproof and can be deployed and recovered over land or water.

At over 1m (4ft) in length and with a wingspan of over 2m (9ft), the Puma is considerably larger than the Raven UAS but can still be hand-launched by a single operator while another operates the ground control station (GCS). The AeroVironment common ground control system is interchangeable between its various UAS systems. The Puma fills a gap between the Raven and much larger systems such as the Predator and Reaper. The Puma can either be operated manually by the controller or set to operate autonomously through GPS navigation.

Standard surveillance equipment for the Puma includes a stabilized electro-

RQ-20 PUMA
A sailor aboard USNS Spearhead Joint High-Speed Vessel (JHSV-1) launches a Puma small unmanned aircraft system (SUAS). The Puma is fitted with an enhanced precision navigation system and is capable of either manual or autonomous flight.

optical (EO) and infrared (IR) camera set in a gimbal system. The Puma has a modular payload system that allows it to be adapted to different mission requirements. This includes an optional under-wing transit bay.

The Puma system is delivered as three air vehicles and two ground stations. It can operate in extreme temperatures and the Puma AE has a reinforced fuselage, making it more robust for mission deployment and recovery. A digital data bank enables the Puma to communicate through sight, voice, video, data and text from

beyond line of sight. Its GPS navigation system enables the Puma to land within 25m (80ft) of a designated land spot, using deep-stall techniques to minimize the impact on the airframe on landing.

Lockheed Martin RQ-170 Sentinel

The RQ-170 Sentinel is a stealth unmanned aerial vehicle that was developed by the Lockheed Martin Skunk Works Advanced Development Program. Details about the Sentinel remain partly shrouded in secrecy and there is a measure of conjecture about its capabilities. Thought to have been originally developed for the Central Intelligence Agency (CIA), the Sentinel is operated by US Air Force

ground controllers and support personnel. Although primarily designed for reconnaissance and surveillance, the Sentinel is thought to have the capacity to carry munitions as well, according to mission requirements.

The Sentinel is flown by US Air Force Air Combat Command 432nd Wing at Creek Air Force Base, Nevada, and by 30th Reconnaissance Squadron, based at Tanopan Test Range, Nevada. The Sentinel was deployed to Afghanistan in 2007 and to South Korea in 2009.

The Sentinel has a flying-wing design and has the appearance of a stealth aircraft. It is equipped with an electro-optical infrared sensor and may also include an

RQ-170 SENTINEL

A captured RQ-170 Sentinel UAV on show at the IRGC aerospace show in Tehran. The Sentinel carries highly sensitive communications interception equipment.

RQ-170 SENTINEL SPECIFICATIONS

Weight:
N/A
Dimensions:
L: 4.5m (14ft 9in); Wingspan: 11.58m (38ft)
Powerplant:
Turbofan
Range/Endurance:
5–6 hours
Service ceiling:
15,240m (50,000ft)
Speed:
N/A
Weapons:
N/A

RQ-170 SENTINEL

Country of origin:
United States
Manufacturer:
Lockheed Martin
Operators:
US Air Force
First flight:
2007

active electronically scanned array (AESA) radar. In view of its stealth configuration, the aircraft is also thought to be capable of carrying highly sensitive equipment for communications interception as well as hyperspectral sensors designed to detect nuclear weapons facilities. A Sentinel is thought to have been deployed during the assault on Osama bin Laden's compound where its communications assets would have aided the covert mission in Pakistani airspace.

Lockheed Martin Stalker

The Stalker is a hand-launched unmanned aerial vehicle designed primarily for reconnaissance, surveillance and target acquisition. It was developed by Lockheed

Martin's Skunk Works advanced projects facility for United States Special Operations Command (USSOCOM).

The Stalker is a fixed-wing aircraft and has a T-tail at the end of a long shaft. It is launched by a bungee-cord ground launching system and it lands on an underbody skid. The Stalker system consists of two aircraft, a command and control ground station, fuel cells and a propane fuel storage tank as well as support equipment. It is operated and controlled by two operators.

The Stalker is fitted with a modular dual electro-optical infrared low-light imaging camera on its belly with a pan, tilt and zoom capability. This can provide both day and night images. The information sent

STALKER XE25

A Marine from 1st Battalion 3rd Marines prepares to launch a Stalker XE25 during a training exercise in California. The Stalker is used by both the US Marine Corps and US Special Operations Command.

back by the Stalker is picked up by a laptop ground control system whereby the operator can control the information and the mission.

An improved version of the Stalker was launched in 2013 with the designation XE. This features greater endurance over the target area as well as a more rugged airframe in order to withstand multiple missions.

MQ-19 Aerosonde

The MQ-19 is an unmanned aerial system (UAS) designed to provide reconnaissance, surveillance and data collection in all weathers and over both land and sea, in day or night operations. Its mission equipment includes full-motion video, communications array and signals intelligence as well as additional mission-specific equipment.

The MQ-19 has a fuselage at the back of which is a Lycoming EL-005 heavy fuel engine with a two-bladed push propeller. It has straight wings and the tailplane is fixed to the end of two extended tubular booms.

The Aerosonde is delivered as a system that includes three aircraft, a launch and recovery trailer and a ground control system. The aircraft is launched on a sliding frame system that gives it the initial boost for take-off while recovery is through a net suspended between two poles. The most advanced versions of the MQ-19 incorporate launch and recovery features. It is also designed to comply with the NATO 4886 One System ground control station and One System remote video terminal arrangements.

The Aerosonde MQ-19 was selected for US Special Operation Command's Mid-Endurance II programme and it has been proven to be reliable in extreme temperatures, including Arctic and desert environments. It has also operated successfully over both land and water. It has good covert characteristics for special operations use, such as low visual and auditory signature. It has the ability to carry multi-intelligence (multi-INT) equipment, including

MQ-19 AEROSONDE

Country of origin:
United States
Manufacturer:
Aerosonde AAI
Operators:
US Special Operations Command;
US Army
First flight:
2021

MQ-19 AEROSONDE SPECIFICATIONS

Weight:
86.4kg (80lb)
Dimensions:
Wingspan: 3.7m (12ft)
Powerplant:
Lycoming EL-005 heavy fuel engine
Range/Endurance:
14+ hours
Service ceiling:
14,572m (15,000ft)
Speed:
83–120km/h (45–65 knots)
Weapons:
N/A

MQ-19 AEROSONDE

An Aerosonde small unmanned aerial system (SUAS) being launched from USS *Gunston Hall*.

electronic warfare (EW) and communications.

Special operations commanders are able to deploy a wide variety of equipment on the MQ-19, depending on mission requirements. These include synthetic aperture radar (SAR), 3D mapping, automatic identification systems and combined electro-optical (EO) and infrared (IR).

Black Hornet Personal Reconnaissance System (PRS)

The Black Hornet PRS is a micro unmanned aerial vehicle (UAV) that can be carried and deployed by individual operators. The Black Hornet system includes two aerial vehicles along with a control station and data receiver. The system can be carried by the operator on a belt or in a pack.

The Black Hornet is designed in the form of a miniature helicopter with a main rotor and a tail rotor. The UAV carries three cameras in the front, with one pointing forward, another pointing down and another set at 45°. The two UAVs allow the operator to fly one while the other is being recharged. The full-motion or still images sent out by the Black Hornet are sent to the handheld receiver whereas the data is stored in the operator's terminal.

The Black Hornet is designed to provide personal and unit reconnaissance mainly in

BLACK HORNET PRS

Country of origin:
Norway/United Kingdom

Manufacturer:
Prox Dynamics/Marlborough Communications Ltd

Operators:
British Army; US Army; US Marine Corps Special Operations Command

First flight:
2006

BLACK HORNET PRS

The Black Hornet personal reconnaissance system (PRS) provides individual users with beyond-line-of-sight situational and threat awareness. This gives elite and special forces operators an added advantage before engaging the enemy.

BLACK HORNET PRS SPECIFICATIONS

Weight:
16g (0.5oz)

Dimensions:
L: 120mm (4.7in)

Powerplant:
Battery powered motor

Range/Endurance:
1.9km (1.2mi)

Service ceiling:
N/A

Speed:
6 m/sec (20 ft/sec) ground speed

Weapons:
N/A

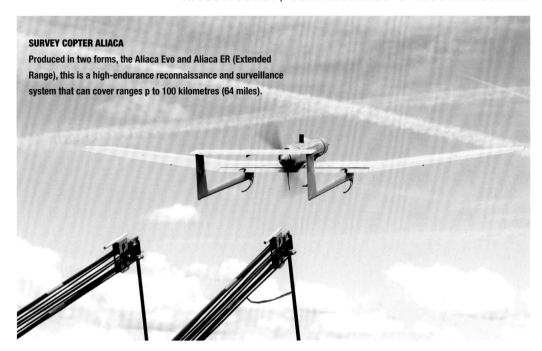

SURVEY COPTER ALIACA
Produced in two forms, the Aliaca Evo and Aliaca ER (Extended Range), this is a high-endurance reconnaissance and surveillance system that can cover ranges p to 100 kilometres (64 miles).

close proximity to the operator. In practical terms, this can include providing vision around or over obstacles such as walls or buildings, looking round corners and even flying down corridors to pre-empt any form of ambush. It can provide information on potential targets as well as post-strike assessment. It is as useful in the field as it is in urban warfare. The Black Hornet can be controlled manually by the operator or it can be pre-set to fly a predetermined route using GPS.

A revised version of the Black Hornet released in 2014 included a night-vision capability as well as long-wave and infrared and video sensors. From a range of up to one mile

from the operator, the Black Hornet is capable of streaming video or high-resolution still images via a data link.

The Black Hornet was issued to British forces such as the Brigade Reconnaissance Force and was deployed in Afghanistan. In 2014, the Black Hornet was selected by the US Army for its Cargo Pocket Intelligence, Surveillance and Reconnaissance (CP-ISR) programme. In 2015, an improved version was tested by special forces and it was also deployed by US Marine Corps Special Operations teams. It was part of the Soldier Borne Sensors (SBS) programme.

In 2018, the Black Hornet 3 was introduced and by 2020 this version was deployed to support

the US Army platoon and unit surveillance reconnaissance.

Survey Copter Aliaca
This electrically powered mini-UAV is designed to perform intelligence, surveillance and reconnaissance (ISR) missions, coastal surveillance and convoy protection, among other tasks. It is fitted with a gyro-stabilized camera. The French Navy placed an order for 11 Aliaca systems.

Desert Hawk (III, IV and EER)
The Desert Hawk small unmanned air system (SUAS) is designed to provide intelligence, reconnaissance, surveillance, target acquisition and similar information to small military units on the ground. The main

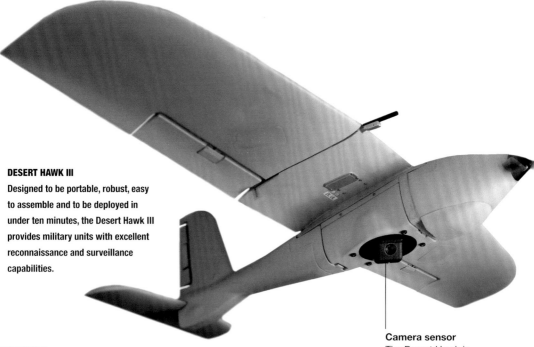

DESERT HAWK III
Designed to be portable, robust, easy to assemble and to be deployed in under ten minutes, the Desert Hawk III provides military units with excellent reconnaissance and surveillance capabilities.

Camera sensor
The Desert Hawk is equipped with a 360° colour optic and full-motion video camera.

DESERT HAWK (III, IV, EER) SPECIFICATIONS

Weight:
3.7kg (8.2lb) (III, IV);
8.6kg (18lb) (EER)

Dimensions:
L: 0.86m (34in); Wingspan:
1.32m (52in)

Powerplant:
Electric engine

Range/Endurance:
1.5 hours (III), 2.5 hours (IV),
2 hours (EER)

Service ceiling:
150m (492ft)

Speed:
92km/h (57mph)

Weapons:
N/A

advantages of the Desert Hawk are its portability, ruggedness and adaptability. Designed to be launched by hand or with the aid of a bungee, it can land without undercarriage. The flexible damage-resistant fuselage is made from a tough polypropylene compound and is also designed to break in such a way as to preserve intact the sensitive electronic equipment on board.

The original version of the Desert Hawk was designed for the US Air Force, Force Protection Airborne Surveillance System (FPASS) programme. The Desert Hawk was also adopted by the 32nd Royal Artillery regiment of the British Army. The Desert Hawk carries 360° colour electro-optic and infrared full-motion video (FMV) camera systems. It can also carry interchangeable snap-on plug-and-play payloads. This makes it a useful asset for a wide range of applications, including day or night small unit support and force protection. The Desert Hawk can be assembled and launched in under 10 minutes.

Lockheed Martin continued to develop the Desert Hawk and in due course a more robust, longer and lighter version designated Desert Hawk III was produced.

DESERT HAWK (III, IV, EER)

Country of origin:

United States

Manufacturer:

Lockheed Martin

Operators:

US Air Force, British Army

First flight:

2003

This version was used widely by US and British forces, including on deployment in Afghanistan. On the new version, the engine and propeller were moved to the front of the aircraft. A further development known as Desert Hawk IV incorporated the latest technological advances without sacrificing weight advantages. It also featured a deep-stall facility to make it easier to land and recover the aircraft. The Desert Hawk IV is capable of flying in extreme weather conditions, including heavy rain, snow and high winds. A larger version of the Desert Hawk, known as Desert Hawk Extended Endurance and Range (DH EER) features a much larger wingspan, giving it greater gliding ability and longer endurance. This enables it to match the larger Tier 2 UAVs while preserving the cost-benefits of Tier 1. The flat-wing surfaces also feature solar power battery regeneration. The DH EER can carry more equipment to enhance signal intelligence (SIGINT) and communications intelligence (COMINT).

Watchkeeper WK450

Developed and built in the United Kingdom, the Watchkeeper is an unmanned aircraft system designed for intelligence, surveillance, target acquisition and reconnaissance (ISTAR). The UAS has the capability to collect, process and disseminate high-quality images. The information gathered by Watchkeeper can either be sent to senior commanders and intelligence analysts or it can provide direct streaming images to soldiers on the ground. This includes imagery of enemy assets and their movements. The Watchkeeper can be effective to a distance of up to 200km (124mi) and can operate at an altitude of 4,876m (16,000ft).

WATCHKEEPER WK450

A Watchkeeper UAV of 47th Regiment Royal Artillery ready for flight at RAF Akrotiri in Cyprus. The Watchkeeper provides target designation for artillery units.

Typically, it can remain airborne for up to four hours.

The Watchkeeper carries an HD electro-optical infrared and laser system as well as a Thales I-Master synthetic aperture radar (SAR), which can be operated in both strip-map and spotlight modes while also supporting high-quality mapping. The Watchkeeper also caries a laser sub-system that incorporates a target marker, designator and rangefinder that can be used to identify different targets through a ground moving target indicator (GMTI). The Watchkeeper can be assigned new tasks while it is still airborne.

The Watchkeeper was developed for the British Army and is operated by 47th Regiment Royal Artillery. It was deployed to Camp Bastion in Afghanistan where it was also deployed with other aerial assets such as the Reaper UAV.

Although it had several developmental problems and suffered some crashes due to software failures, the Watchkeeper was due for a mid-life extension from 2026, which would include the replacement of obsolete components. Improvements to the aircraft and its control systems were to be overseen by the British Army Intelligence, Surveillance, Targeting, Acquisition and Reconnaissance (ISTAR) office.

Piaggio P.1HH Hammerhead UAS

Based on the airframe of the P.180 Avanti business turboprop, the P.1HH Hammerhead is a high-end, medium-altitude long-endurance (MALE) unmanned aircraft system (UAS) designed primarily for intelligence, surveillance and reconnaissance (ISR) missions. As it is based on a manned passenger aircraft, the P.1HH has plenty of space for on-board equipment as well as fuel cells for long endurance missions. The twin Pratt and Whitney Canada turboprops with five-blade low-noise propellers provide significant pusher thrust to make this the fastest MALE UAS in its class. The equipment packages onboard the Hammerhead can be adapted to mission priorities, including ISR, communications intelligence (COMINT), electronics intelligence (ELINT) and signals intelligence (SIGINT). These are controlled through a mission management system (MMS). The control of the aircraft itself is via a vehicle control management system (VCMS).

Communications from the ground control station are via an airborne data link system that includes line of sight (LOS) and beyond line of sight (BLOS) data links. The ground control station includes a flight control crew and all the

P.1HH HAMMERHEAD

A Hammerhead medium-altitude long-endurance (MALE) unmanned aerial vehicle (UAV) at the International Defence Exhibition (IDEX) in Abu Dhabi in 2015. The Hammerhead is adapted from the P.180 Avanti business aircraft.

necessary equipment to control up to three unmanned aircraft systems.

The UAS also features automatic take-off and landing (ATOL). A shielded flight deck and a dorsal fairing indicate the areas where the SATCOM

P.1HH HAMMERHEAD

Country of origin:

Italy

Manufacturer:

Piaggio Aerospace

Operators:

United Arab Emirates

First flight:

2013

P.1HH HAMMERHEAD SPECIFICATIONS

Weight:

6,600kg (14,500lb)

Dimensions:

L: 14.4m (49ft 2in);

Wingspan: 18,00m² (193.75ft²)

Powerplant:

Pratt & Whitney Canada 850 SHP

Range/Endurance:

8,149km (5,063mi)

Service ceiling:

13,716m (45,000ft)

Speed:

731km/h (454mph)

Weapons:

N/A

system, avionics and mission-related equipment are housed.

In an increasingly competitive market for MALE UAS systems, the Hammerhead is a high-specification contender as a converted passenger aircraft whereas most of the competition are purpose-built UAS designs.

Denel Dynamics Bateleur

This medium-altitude long-endurance (MALE) unmanned aerial vehicle (UAV) is designed for surveillance and signals intelligence. Its design is comparable to the General Atomics MQ-1 Predator-A UAV. It has a bulbous nose area that houses the avionics as well as sensors. The optics are set in a rotating gimbal under the nose. The straight wings are mounted midway along the fuselage and horizontal tailplanes support vertical tail fins. The engine is situated at the rear of the fuselage and powers a three-blade propeller. The Bateleur has a modular construction that allows for different configurations and the UAV can be broken down and transported in a container. The Bateleur can carry a variety of equipment including a Denel Optronics Argos-410 electro-optical (EO) infrared (IR) system with optional laser rangefinder, a laser designator, an electronics emitter locating system, electronic intelligence equipment and a synthetic aperture radar (SAR). The UAV is capable of electronic intelligence (ELINT), communications intelligence (COMINT), airborne communications relay and photo reconnaissance, target location and designation, battlefield surveillance and artillery fire support.

Falco Explorer

The Explorer is a medium-altitude long-endurance (MALE) unmanned aerial vehicle (UAV) designed to provide persistent intelligence, surveillance and reconnaissance. It has the capacity to carry a broad range of both standard and mission-specific sensors. The Falco has an extended fuselage with a raised area at the front end and a v-shaped tail, behind which is a pusher propeller driven by a conventional aircraft engine. The aircraft is fitted with retractable landing gear. The Falco is delivered as a system that features a ground control station, a ground data terminal,

two aircraft and support equipment. The system can be delivered in air-transportable containers.

The basic package carried by the Falco includes multifunctional synthetic aperture radar, an electro-optical multi-sensor gyro-stabilized turret and a signals intelligence suite. It carries a Gabiano T8OUL surveillance radar for mapping, ground moving target indication (GMTI) and search and rescue (SAR) operations.

The flying capabilities and equipment packages of the Falco make it a useful military asset while also enabling its use in homeland security and search and rescue (SAR). The aircraft can also be used for maritime surveillance. The Falco's lightweight electro-optical space sensor (EOSS) turret houses up to eight sensors including infrared (IR) and visual cameras, laser rangefinder, laser illuminator and laser designator. The aircraft also carries SAGE electronic intelligence (ELINT), signals intelligence (SIGINT) sensors and climactic identification systems.

FALCO EXPLORER

A Falco Explorer at the International Paris Air Show at Le Bourget in 2019. The LEOSS multi-sensor optics system is located in a 4-axes gyro-stabilized turret system. The turret contains up to six electro-optical (EO) sensors.

Other types of equipment can be carried according to mission requirements.

The Falco is fitted with an automatic and assisted flight management system that manages automatic take-off and landing.

ORBITER 2 SPECIFICATIONS

Weight:

1,500kg (3,306lb)

Dimensions:

Wingspan: 3m (9.8ft)

Powerplant:

Wingspan: 3m (9.8ft)

Range/Endurance:

100km (62mi) / 4 hours

Service ceiling:

N/A

Speed:

129.5km/h (70 knots, 80.5mph)

Weapons:

N/A

Orbiter 2, 3 and 4

The Orbiter small unmanned aerial reconnaissance vehicles are produced in three different versions, 2, 3 and 4, each one being larger and more capable than the other.

Orbiter 2

The smallest version, the Orbiter 2 is a light man-portable unmanned aerial system (MUAS) designed for intelligence gathering,

surveillance, target acquisition and reconnaissance (ISTAR). This MUAS can be used for both high and low intensity warfare, urban warfare and counterinsurgency. It can also be used for maritime surveillance. It can perform both day and night operations and features stabilized electro-optical (IR) and infrared (IR) sensors; an EO camera with laser designator; and photogrammetric mapping.

ORBITER 2

This compact lightweight mini-UAV is designed for tactical real-time intelligence, surveillance and target acquisition (ISTAR) missions. It can be carried and launched by a single operator.

The MUAS is launched by catapult and features automatic take-off and landing. It is recovered by parachute over land and by a net when at sea.

ORBITER 2

Country of origin:

Israel

Manufacturer:

Aeronautics Group

Operators:

Irish Army; Azerbaijani Land Forces; Mexican Federal Police; Israeli Sea Corps; Polish Army; Finnish Army and Serbian Army

First flight:

2008

Orbiter 3

The Orbiter 3 is a small tactical unmanned aerial vehicle (STUAV) that carries multiple sensors. The Orbiter 3 provides long-endurance intelligence, surveillance, target acquisition and reconnaissance (ISTAR). It also features a digital data link and laser target designation. It also has signals intelligence (SIGINT) capabilities. The Orbiter 3 can be deployed in seven minutes from a catapult and its electrical engine has a low noise signature to complement its low silhouette for covert operations. The Orbiter 3 is a robust, combat-proven platform with a wide range of applications.

ORBITER 3

An Orbiter 3 UAV and control module at the unmanned vehicles conference in Tel Aviv in 2015. The display on the ruggedized laptop shows the sort of real-time intelligence that a UAV can obtain.

ORBITER 4
SPECIFICATIONS

Weight:

12kg (26.4lb)

Dimensions:

Wingspan: 5.5m (18ft)

Powerplant:

Multi-fuel spark-ignited engine

Range/Endurance:

24 hours

Service ceiling:

5486m (18,000ft)

Speed:

129.5km/h (70 knots, 80.1mph)

Weapons:

N/A

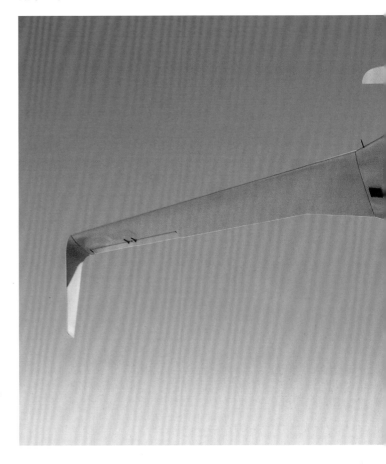

ORBITER 4

The Orbiter 4 is an enhanced version of the Orbiter 3 and is particularly suited to maritime operations. It can be operated from a wide range of vessels to provide target acquisition and fire direction.

ORBITER 4

Country of origin:

Israel

Manufacturer:

Aeronautics Group

Operators:

Israeli Defense Forces

First flight:

2008

Orbiter 4

The Orbiter 4 has all the features of the Orbiter 3 along with further enhancements. It has greater endurance and operational flexibility, more advanced avionics and a wider range of tactical applications. It is capable of both land and maritime intelligence, surveillance, target acquisition and reconnaissance (ISTAR), communications intelligence (COMINT) and electronic warfare (EW). Its advanced image processing capabilities include an automatic video tracker, digital zoom and super-resolution, video motion detection (VMD), video mosaic composition and D-roll and image stabilization. Unlike the Orbiters 2 and 3, the Orbiter 4 has a spark-ignited multi-fuel engine. It features automatic take-off and landing and has six autonomous flight modes. Maritime uses include deep-sea and coastal reconnaissance and it can be used on a wide variety of naval vessels.

Dominator XP

This medium-altitude long-endurance (MALE) unmanned aerial system (UAS) is based on the Austrian Demon DA-42 Twin Star manned aircraft. It is designed primarily for all-weather intelligence, surveillance and reconnaissance (ISR), as well as maritime surveillance and homeland security.

Its multi-sensor, multi-mission system incorporates data link, line-of-sight (LOS) and beyond-line-of-sight (BLOS), as well as satellite communications (SATCOM). The variable mission-related equipment load may include electro-optical (EO), infrared (IR) and hyperspectral sensors; a laser pointer and designator; maritime radar; SAR/GMTI radars and communications relays. It can operate up to 300km (186mi) on a line-of-sight (LOS) data link, but can also be fitted with satellite communications (SATCOM) for beyond-line-of-sight (BLOS) operations, using geostationary satellites. The system includes a ground station with a user-friendly interface that is used for route planning, operational modes, sensor control and target designation.

The Dominator is capable of maritime anti-submarine and anti-ship operations. The UAS is also fitted with an automatic launch and recovery (ALR) system. The aircraft is capable of maintaining straight and level flight, even should one of the engines fail. The Dominator meets the requirements of the

DOMINATOR XP
SPECIFICATIONS

Weight:

1,200kg (2,640lb)

Dimensions:

L: 8.6m (28ft 2in); Wingspan: 13.5m (44ft

3in); H 2.5m (8ft 2in)

Powerplant:

2 Thielert diesel engines

Range/Endurance:

20 hours

Service ceiling:

9,100m (30,000ft)

Speed:

354km/h (219mph)

Weapons:

N/A

DOMINATOR XP

Based on a conventional
light passenger aircraft, the
Dominator XP is capable
of carrying a wide range of
payloads, providing strategic
intelligence and surveillance
for both land and maritime
operations.

DOMINATOR XP

Country of origin:

Israel

Manufacturer:

Aeronautics Group

Operators:

Israeli Defense Force (IDF)

First flight:

2009

AEROSTAR

The Aerostar tactical UAV is a combat-proven system that is deployed by military forces worldwide. Its large payload bay can carry a wide array of sensors and radar.

AEROSTAR SPECIFICATIONS

Weight:
100kg (220lb)

Dimensions:
L: 4.5m (14ft 9in); Wingspan: 7.5m (24ft 7in); H: 1.3m (4ft 3in)

Powerplant:
2-stroke Zanzoterra 498i boxed engine

Range/Endurance:
200km (124mi) / 12 hours

Service ceiling:
5,486m (18,000ft)

Speed:
203km/h (126mph)

Weapons:
N/A

Israeli Defence Force (IDF) and has been deployed by some NATO members.

Aerostar

The Aerostar tactical unmanned aerial system (TUAS) is a tried and tested system that has accumulated about 250,000 flight hours in operations worldwide. The Aerostar can support multiple payloads in a flexible system that can be adapted to mission requirements. The Aerostar has a high wing in the upper part of the fuselage and a diesel engine at the rear powers a pusher propeller. Two parallel booms extend to the rear to support the rear tailplane assembly, with two vertical tailplanes supporting a horizontal tailplane. An electro-optic gimbal camera is located midway along the belly of the fuselage while a mast on the top of the fuselage supports the data link system.

The Aerostar can carry out GPS/INS navigation and targeting, navigation in GPS-denied areas, an automatic take-off and landing (ATOC) system and programmable autonomous flight modes. Equipment includes EO/IR sensors, a laser designator, synthetic aperture radars (SAR/GMTI) and electronic intelligence sensors.

The whole array of equipment enables the Aerostar to carry out land and maritime ISTAR, electronic warfare, force protection and target acquisition. Intelligence

AEROSTAR

Country of origin:
Israel
Manufacturer:
Aeronautics Group
Operators:
Israel Defense Force (IDF)
First flight:
2000

is transferred to the ground station via a satellite communication data link.

Hermes 450

This combat-proven unmanned aerial vehicle (UAV) is designed for long-endurance missions and is capable of carrying multiple payloads, including dual payload configurations that allow it to carry out two concurrent missions. The

Hermes 450 has a long tubular fuselage with straight wings. A Wankel four-stroke engine drives a two-bladed propeller at the rear of the fuselage and it features two canted tailplanes in a V-shape. The Hermes 450 has a fixed undercarriage. A gimbal under the fuselage carries the optics systems. The Hermes 450 can carry a range of sensors including an electro-optic (EO) and infrared (IR) laser and ground moving target indicator (GMTI) and it is capable of communications intelligence (COMINT), signals intelligence (SIGINT) and electronics intelligence (ELINT). It also carries hyperspectral systems. It features an automatic take-off and landing system and is highly autonomous.

The Hermes 450 has been used in combat by the Israel

HERMES 450 SPECIFICATIONS

Weight:
550kg (1212lb)
Dimensions:
L: 6.10m (20ft); Wingspan: 10.5m (34.4ft)
Powerplant:
Wankel 4-stroke engine
Range/Endurance:
260km (124m) / 17 hours
Service ceiling:
5,486m (18,000ft)
Speed:
176km/h (109mph)
Weapons:
N/A

HERMES 450

The Hermes 450 is a combat-proven tactical UAV widely used by the Israeli Defense Forces and by other military forces worldwide. It was deployed by British forces in Afghanistan and forms the basis of the UK Watchkeeper UAV.

HERMES 900

**With persistent surveillance capabilities
and long endurance, the Hermes 900 can
detect both ground and maritime targets
over a wide spectral range.**

Defense Force (IDF) and has
been deployed by the armed
forces of several nations. The
British Army's Watchkeeper
UAV is a development of the
Hermes 450 and was used
extensively by the British Army
in Afghanistan.

Hermes 900

The Hermes 900 is a medium-
altitude long-endurance (MALE)
unarmed aerial vehicle (UAV)
designed for intelligence,

surveillance, target acquisition
and reconnaissance (ISTAR)
missions. It is equipped with
a variety of sensors, including
electro-optical (EO) and
infrared (IR) sensors; synthetic
aperture radar; ground
moving target indication;
communications and electronic
intelligence; electronic warfare
capabilities and hyperspectral
sensors. It also carries satellite
communication and a line-of-
sight (LOS) data link and has

HERMES 900

Country of origin:
Israel
Manufacturer:
Elbit Systems
Operators:
Israeli Air Force (IAF)
First flight:
2009

HERMES 900 SPECIFICATIONS

Weight:
830kg (1,830lb)
Dimensions:
L: 8.3m (27ft 2in);
Wingspan: 15m(49ft 2in)
Powerplant:
Rotax 914 engine
Range/Endurance:
40 hours
Service ceiling:
9,144m (30,000ft)
Speed:
222km/h (138mph)
Weapons:
N/A

adverse weather capabilities. A bulged area at the front of the airframe houses avionics and other operational systems. The system is operated from a universal ground control station (UGCS), which can also be used to control the Hermes 450 UAV. The Hermes 900 is powered by a Rotax engine driving a pusher propeller at the rear and it has hardpoints in the main wings for spare fuel tanks. It features a retractable undercarriage, thus reducing drag in flight. The Hermes 900 has been ordered by the Israeli Air Force (IAF) and is also under consideration by other national forces including the Royal Thai Navy.

Hermes 45

This multi-mission, small tactical unarmed aircraft system (STUAS) is designed for intelligence, surveillance, target acquisition and reconnaissance (ISTAR) at brigade and division level. It can also be employed for maritime missions. The Hermes 45 is launched from a catapult and is recovered using an automated spot landing sequence. It has a line-of-sight range of 200km (124mi) with satellite communications (SATCOM). An internal payload bay can house a range of equipment including electro-optic (EO) and infrared (IR), marine radar, a terrain dominance sensor, electronic intelligence (ELINT), communications intelligence (COMINT) and other options.

Heron Mk II

The Heron Mk II is distinguished from the Heron Mk I by its longer and wider fuselage and more powerful engine that increases the climb rate by 50 per cent. The Mk II version also has a stand-off capability that enables it to gather intelligence without crossing international borders or coming within range of hostile weaponry. This is made possible by more powerful sensors.

Heron Mk I

This medium-altitude long-endurance (MALE) unmanned aerial system (UAS) is designed for both tactical and strategic missions. Capable of reaching altitudes of up to 35,000ft, it can stay airborne for up to 45 hours. The Heron's multi-mission system incorporates a variety of equipment that enables it to carry out intelligence, surveillance, target acquisition and reconnaissance (ISTAR) over both land and

HERMES 45 SPECIFICATIONS

Weight:
70kg (154lb)

Dimensions:
L: 1m (3ft 3in); Wingspan: 5m (16ft 4in); H: 0.8m (2ft 7in)

Powerplant:
N/A

Range/Endurance:
200km (124mi) / 22 hours

Service ceiling:
5,486m (18,000ft)

Speed:
N/A

Weapons:
N/A

HERMES 45

Designed for point launch and recovery from either land or naval vessels, the Hermes 45 is a compact system that offers a wide array of reconnaissance, surveillance and targeting capabilities.

HERON MK I

Designed for strategic reconnaissance and surveillance operations, the Heron Mk I is a highly successful platform that is in service with military forces worldwide. It can interact with ground, air and maritime forces.

sea. It can use both direct line-of-sight (LOS) and beyond-line-of-sight (BLOS) through satellite communications to send back data to the operators in real time. On-board equipment includes synthetic aperture radar (SAR), communications intelligence (COMINT), electronic support measures (ESM) and electronic intelligence (ELINT) as well as maritime patrol radar (MPR). A heavy fuel version of the Mk 1 is called the Super Heron HF.

Heron TP

The Heron TP is an advanced long-range MALE UAS. It is longer, faster and can achieve higher altitudes than

HERON MK I

Country of origin:
Italy
Manufacturer:
Leonardo
Operators:
Various
First flight:
2020

HERON MK I SPECIFICATIONS

Weight:
70kg (154lb)
Dimensions:
L: 1m (3ft 3in); Wingspan:
5m (16ft 4in); H: 0.8m (2ft 7in)
Powerplant:
N/A
Range/Endurance:
200km (124mi) / 22 hours
Service ceiling:
5,486m (18,000ft)
Speed:
N/A
Weapons: N/A

the Heron Mk I and includes automatic take-off and landing systems (ATOL) and satellite communications (SATCOM). It can perform intelligence, surveillance, target acquisition and reconnaissance (ISTAR) while being adaptable to a range of mission requirements.

TACTICAL HERON SPECIFICATIONS

Weight:
N/A

Dimensions:
L: 7.3m (23ft 11in); Wingspan: 10.6m (34ft 9in)

Powerplant:
Rotax fuel injection engine

Range/Endurance:
300km (186mi) / 24 hours

Service ceiling:
7,010 (23,000ft)

Speed:
222km/h (120ktas, 138mph)

Weapons:
N/A

Tactical Heron

The smallest platform in the Heron family, the Tactical Heron is a multi-million, multi-payload tactical unmanned aerial system (TUAS). Despite its relatively small size, the Tactical Heron is also the most powerful tactical system in the IAI inventory, featuring the latest technology. It can gather intelligence and transmit it in real time to its military operators. The UAS features a wide band, data link that can easily be upgraded with beyond-line-of-sight (BLOS) using satellite communications (SATCOM). The Tactical Heron is also designed to be highly practical and it can be deployed from semi-prepared airfields. It is also interoperable with other IAI systems, including the ground control system (GCS).

The equipment carried on the Tactical Heron includes synthetic aperture radar (SAR), communications intelligence

TACTICAL HERON
An IAI Heron Unmanned Aerial Vehicle takes off the runway at Palmachim Air Force Base, Israel.

TACTICAL HERON

Country of origin:
Israel

Manufacturer:
IAI Malat

Operators:
Israel Defense Forces (IDF)

First flight:
2019

(COMINT), electronic support measures (ESM) and electronic intelligence (ELINT). It also carries maritime patrol radar (MPR).

Searcher

The Searcher is a multi-mission, tactical unarmed aerial system (TUAS) with a primary role of intelligence, surveillance, target acquisition and reconnaissance (ISTAR). It can also perform artillery adjustment and damage assessment missions. Although it is over twice the size of the Scout, the Searcher is still a compact system that can provide high-quality, real-time intelligence gathering and transmission while operating from a stand-off position.

The equipment carried by the Searcher typically includes synthetic aperture radar (SAR), communications intelligence (COMINT), electronic support measures (ESM), electronic intelligence (ELINT), maritime patrol radar (MPR) and other mission-related equipment.

A Russian version of the Searcher, the Forpost-R, was used by Russian forces during the war in Ukraine in 2022. The Searcher is also used by the armed forces of India, Thailand, South Korea, Turkey and Spain.

IAI Ranger

The Ranger was developed by IAI in association with RUAG Aviation for Swiss military requirements and with special design features to improve survivability and optimum efficiency in extreme weather conditions. The Ranger is launched from a hydraulic catapult whereas its skid landing system enables it to land on rugged landing strips, whether they are grass or covered in snow or ice. The Ranger has been in service with both the Swish Air Force and Finnish Defence Forces.

Bayraktar Mini UAV

The Bayraktar Mini unmanned aerial vehicle is the first unmanned aircraft system to be produced by Baykar and also the first Turkish-produced air system to be deployed by the Turkish armed forces. The Mini UAV is a highly portable system designed for short-range day and night aerial reconnaissance at squad level. The air system is made from composite fibre Kevlar and is designed to be easily assembled and launched.

The ground control system is also easily portable. The system incorporates automatic take-off and landing, a waypoint management system and automated tracking. It also features automatic target point tracking and a digital communications system. If there is a loss of communications with the ground control station (GCS), the UAV will return home and land automatically. This is in addition to the automatic take-off and cruise system. The UAV carries a gimbal underneath the fuselage. It usually performs a skid landing but can also be retrieved by parachute. The UAV has been produced in three versions, Mini A, Mini B and Mini D. The Mini D has twice the communications range of its predecessors and is capable of three times the altitude.

Eleron-3 (Aileron-3)

This small, short-range, unmanned aerial vehicle is designed to provide reconnaissance and surveillance for troops on the frontline. The UAV can carry out autonomous, remote-controlled missions that include area patrols and joint observation. It has an autonomous flight option, GPS navigation and automatic landing. Its modular mission equipment includes a module with an infrared camera and low-light TV camera or

ELERON-3

Russian soldiers launch an Eleron UAV on a military training exercise near Bishkek in 2015. The Eleron-3 has been deployed by Russian forces during the war in Ukraine to provide tactical reconnaissance.

ELERON-3 SPECIFICATIONS

Weight:
MTOW 4.9kg (10.8lb)

Dimensions:
L: 0.6m (1ft 9in); Wingspan: 1.47m (4ft 8in)

Powerplant:
Electric motor

Range/Endurance:
N/A

Service ceiling:
4,000m (13,000ft)

Speed:
130km/h (81mph)

Weapons:
N/A

one with a TV camera and thermal imaging camera. This enables the UAV to deliver real-time battlefield information to operators on the ground. The Eleron-3 has a blended wing and fuselage design. A powerplant is located at the rear of the fuselage with a two-blade propeller. It has an optics gimbal with 360° traverse.

A1-CM Furia

Developed since 2014 by Ukrainian company Athlon-Avia, the A1-CM Furia is a flying-wing unmanned aerial system that can be used for aerial reconnaissance and artillery adjustment. In 2019–20 the A1-CM Furia was officially adopted by Ukrainian armed forces and over 100 systems have been deployed. The system consists of three unmanned aerial vehicles

along with daytime and night-time imaging equipment. The UAV has a semi-automatic guided or autonomous camera-guided flight mode. It also features automatic take-off and landing. Although the flight path of the UAV can be pre-programmed, it can also be altered during flight. The UAV can return to base automatically if there is a communications break with the operator.

The Furia can be operated in a camera-guided flight mode and can also be integrated with an artillery fire-control system. Other features of the Furia include an inertial navigation system, satellite navigation system and on-board navigation lights.

The portable ground control station comes in a ruggedized, shockproof and waterproof

A1-CM FURIA

Country of origin:
Ukraine

Manufacturer:
Athlon-Avia

Operators:
Ukrainian armed forces

First flight:
2014

A1-CM FURIA

A Ukrainian soldier prepares to launch a Fura UAV. The Furia has been used extensively by Ukrainian forces during their defence against the Russian invasion for intelligence, surveillance and reconnaissance (ISR).

case. It has two HD monitors and enables full control of the UAV and on-board equipment by two operators.

Sparrow

The Sparrow unmanned aerial system (UAS) is designed for squad-level aerial reconnaissance at a range of up to 20km (12.4mi). It is ideal for use by special forces, for scouting and reconnaissance and can also be used for artillery spotting and direction. The Sparrow system is designed to be carried by one soldier, including the air vehicle itself, ground control station, antenna and launch system. On return to base,

A1-CM FURIA SPECIFICATIONS

Weight:
5kg (11lb)

Dimensions:
L: 0.90m (3.2ft); Wingspan: 2m (6ft 6in)

Powerplant:
Electric motor

Range/Endurance:
50km/3 hours

Service ceiling:
N/A

Speed:
65km/h (40mph)

Weapons:
N/A

SPARROW

Country of origin:
Spain
Manufacturer:
Spaitech
Operators:
Ukrainian armed forces
First flight:
2020

the Sparrow is recovered by parachute. The design of the Sparrow is a blended flying wing and it carries a gimbal with a 360° traverse under the fuselage. The engine is at the front of the fuselage powering a two-blade propeller. Vertical winglets at the end of the main wings provide improved fuel efficiency and handling. The Sparrow is capable of flying in both land and maritime environments. The Sparrow can fly autonomously and its camera systems provide both still and real-time imagery. It was deployed by Ukrainian forces during the war with Russia in 2022.

Orlan-10

The Orlan-10 is a medium-range unmanned aerial vehicle (UAV) designed for aerial reconnaissance, observation, surveillance, 3D mapping, search and rescue (SAR) and other roles. First produced in 2010, the Orlan-10 has been deployed in several

Russian Reconnaissance Fire UAVs

Russian medium unmanned aerial vehicles, such as the Orlan-10 and Granat-4, are operated by artillery reconnaissance sub-units in the Russian army. The UAVs have been used successfully in forward observation missions and are operated by mini- and short-range UAV platoons in the Brigade UAV company. The UAV operators determine the co-ordinates of a target and relay that information to artillery forward observers who in turn pass it on to the artillery fire-control personnel. When operated successfully, the UAVs can provide accurate firing co-ordinates in real time. The effectiveness of Russian UAVs in this role has also been recognized by their opponents.

During the war in Ukraine, large numbers of Orlan-10 and other Russian UAVs were compromised by jamming or were shot down. The attrition rate is said to have severely degraded the ability of Russian forces to carry out UAV-based reconnaissance and fire missions.

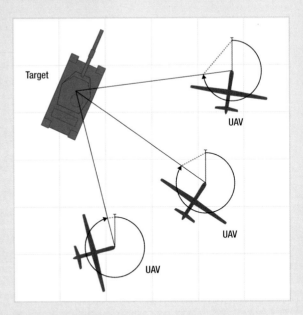

TAKING COORDINATES

UAVs can combine to take several azimuths on a target, which are then deciphered through the use of trigonometry to pinpoint the target for a fire mission.

ORLAN-10

Country of origin:
Russia
Manufacturer:
Russian Special Technology Centre LLC
Operators:
Russian armed forces
First flight:
2014

ORLAN-10

An Orlan-10 UAV and its MP32M1 command vehicle on display in Khabarovsk, Russia in 2021. The Orlan-10 is a simple but effective UAV that has been used by Russian forces during their invasion of Ukraine.

combat zones, including Armenia, Nagorno-Karabakh, Syria, Donbas and the war in Ukraine. The Orlan-10 system includes two aerial vehicles, a ground control station (GCS), a portable launch system and spare parts. The ground control station (GCS) is based inside an MP32M1 command and control vehicle that communicates with the UAV through a digital data link.

The Orlan-10 has a modular design with a high-wing configuration and a tailplane with a vertical stabilizer. The engine is situated at the front of the airframe and drives a two-blade propeller. The UAV is launched from a collapsible catapult and recovered by

ORLAN-10 SPECIFICATIONS

Weight:
9kg (20lb)
Dimensions:
L: 2m (6ft 6in); Wingspan: 3.1m (10ft 2in)
Powerplant:
Petrol engine
Range/Endurance:
150m (93mi)
Service ceiling:
5,000m (16,404ft)
Speed:
150km/h (93mph)
Weapons:
N/A

Skyhawk

The Sky Hawk series of small stealth UAVs produced by China's Aerospace Science and Industry Corporation are designed for reconnaissance and intelligence gathering. Sky Hawk 1, first unveiled in 2018, is a flying-wing design with an engine in the tail driving a pusher propeller.

Sky Hawk 3 has a twin-boom configuration and a piston engine driving a pusher propeller. It features an inverted V-tail plane. Sky Hawk 3A is essentially the same as 3 but has tricycle undercarriage for recovery as well as being slightly heavier. Despite the name, Sky Hawk 3B bears no relation to the 3A. It is a hand-held micro-UAV, which is powered by an electric motor under the wing that drives a two-blade propeller.

an on-board parachute. The interchangeable payloads include a daylight camera, a thermal imaging camera, a video camera and a radio transmitter fitted into a gyro-stabilized camera pod located under the fuselage. Imagery and video are transmitted to the ground control station in real time.

The UAV can carry out missions in either autonomous or remote-control modes. An upgraded model of the Orlan-10 also features a laser designator.

Granat series

The Granat unmanned aerial systems are produced in various sizes and increase in sophistication and range incrementally.

Granat-1

The Granat-1 is a small flying-wing design that can be easily hand-launched. It has a two-blade propeller at the front of the fuselage.

Granat-2

This version, although larger than the Granat-1, can also be hand-launched. It has a more defined fuselage than the Granat-1, straight wings and slanted tailplanes at the end of a tail boom.

Granat-4

The Granat-4 is a medium-range UAS with an engine at the rear of the fuselage powering a pusher propellor. It has straight wings and the tailplane is mounted at the end of a tail boom. This version is launched from a catapult. The Granat 4 system comprises two UAVs, payload modules, a charging

GRANAT-4
The Granat-4 UAV is used for reconnaissance as well as signals intelligence (SIGINT). The Granat-4 is launched from a catapult rail system.

and refuelling station, a ground control station based on the KAMAZ 7350 truck, two transport containers and a collapsible catapult. The Granat-4 is used for reconnaissance and artillery spotting over a range of about 70km (43mi). The latest version of the Granat-4 can carry signals intelligence (SIGINT) payloads that enable it to carry out radio monitoring, signals collection and direction as well as acting as an airborne radio relay station.

Avic WZ-8

The Avic WZ-8 is a supersonic/hypersonic unmanned aerial vehicle (UAV) with similarities in design to the Lockheed D-21 UAV. The UAV is launched from an aircraft and then engages rocket motors to reach high velocities and high altitudes. It can achieve hypersonic speeds at 15,240m (50,000ft). The role of the WZ-8 is general reconnaissance as well as force

WZ-8

A WZ-8 supersonic reconnaissance UAV in Tiananmen Square, Beijing. The hypersonic WZ-8 is designed for reconnaissance, intelligence gathering and target assessment.

assessment and other combat-related intelligence gathering. Where satellite imagery may be compromised, it can overfly areas of interest several times. The UAV is fitted with a tricycle undercarriage for recovery on a runway.

WZ-8

Country of origin:
China
Manufacturer:
Aviation Industry Corporation of China (AVIC)
Operators:
Chinese armed forces
First flight:
2019

WZ-8 SPECIFICATIONS

Weight:
N/A
Dimensions:
L: 20.57m (67ft 5in); Wingspan: 2.85m (9ft 4in); H 3.20m (10.5ft)
Powerplant:
Two rocket boosters
Range/Endurance:
N/A
Service ceiling:
42,675m (14,010ft)
Speed:
5,310km/h (3,294mph)
Weapons:
N/A

UNMANNED COMBAT AERIAL VEHICLES (UCAV)

The unmanned combat aerial vehicle (UCAV) – mostly developed from reconnaissance platforms – has been one of the most significant developments in aerial warfare in the modern age. The evolution of the UCAV is well demonstrated by the General Atomics RQ-1 Predator. Originally conceived as an unarmed reconnaissance platform, it was later armed with missiles and in 2002 was designated the MQ-1 Predator to mark its change of role. The Predator was succeeded by the MQ-1 Reaper which, while it maintained enhanced intelligence, surveillance, reconnaissance and targeting abilities (ISRT), was also a highly developed strike UAV.

While the Predator and Reaper were developed by a superpower, Israel had proved with its Scout, Mastiff, Searcher and Hermes drones that a smaller country could develop highly effective unmanned aerial vehicles both for reconnaissance and strike missions. Soon Turkey joined the club and began to develop some of the most game-changing unmanned combat air vehicles of the 21st century. In 2014, Baykar developed the Bayraktar TB2 UACAV, which would play a leading and decisive role in conflicts that included Libya, Syria, Nagorno-Karabakh and Ukraine.

MQ-9 REAPER

A US Air Force MQ-9 Reaper assigned to the 432nd Wing/432nd Air Expeditionary Wing takes off from the flight line at Creech Air Force Base, Nevada, September 2021.

Protector RG Mk 1

The United Kingdom has ordered a successor to its current MQ-9A Reaper fleet. Designated the Protector RG Mk 1 (MQ-9B), the new version has an improved ISTAR capability. The new aircraft will be fitted with detect-and-avoid technology so that it can operate safely in crowded airspace and will also feature automatic take-off and landing, which will reduce the deployment footprint. Its persistent reconnaissance capability will be enhanced by a high-definition, electro-optical infrared (IR) camera.

War in Ukraine

The war in Ukraine demonstrated the effectiveness of armed drones and how they could tip the balance in favour of a militarily weaker power. In the early weeks of the conflict, Ukrainian Bayraktar TB2 drones had a significant impact on Russian forces and it took some time for Russian air defences to have enough of an attrition rate on the slow low-flying drones to mitigate their effects. However, Ukraine had demonstrated how a country with a smaller conventional manned air force than its opponent could punch above its weight, while also keeping its manned aircraft and pilots out of risk. This point is significant for as manned fighter jets become ever more sophisticated so do even wealthy nations tend to buy fewer of them. As discussed in Chapter 5, drone technology may be harnessed to fill the numbers gap.

BAYRAKTAR TB2 UCAV

Ukrainian servicemen push a Bayraktar TB2 UCAV at the Kulbakyne aerodrome during the Exercise Sea Breeze 2021, Mykolaiv, southern Ukraine.

MQ-9 REAPER

Country of origin:
United States
Manufacturer: General Atomics
Operators: US Air Force; US
Special Operations Command;
Royal Air Force; Spain, France,
Netherlands, Italy
First flight: February 2001

While the United States has limited the supply of its drone technologies to trusted nations (the Predator XP is a limited version of the UAV for export purposes), China has exported drones much more widely.

General Atomics
MQ-9 Reaper

The MQ-9 reaper is a development of the MQ-1 Predator but is so different from its predecessor as to make it seem an entirely new unmanned aerial vehicle (UAV). The MQ-9 is significantly longer and heavier than the Predator

and can carry about fifteen times more ordnance than the Predator. Its cruising speed is also three times faster.

The MQ-9 was designed primarily for intelligence, surveillance and reconnaissance duties but also has the capability for close air support, combat and strike missions. Its unique range of abilities makes it a useful asset for special operations missions. In some ways, the Reaper embodies the transition from the use of UAVs as intelligence-gathering assets to a more pronounced hunter/ killer role.

The Reaper is equipped with a wide array of sensors based on the Raytheon AN/ AAS-52 multi-spectral targeting (MTS) sensor suite, including infrared (IR) sensors, a colour/ monochrome daylight TV camera, an image-intensified TV camera and a laser designator and laser illuminator.

The six stores pylons on the MQ-9 can be fitted with

MQ-9B REAPER
The General Atomics MQ-9B Reaper Unmanned Aerial Vehicle is staged at the US Army Yuma Proving Grounds, US Army Test and Evaluation Command, Yuma, Arizona, November 2019. The Reaper was used for an intelligence, surveillance, target acquisition and reconnaissance mission during the Marine Air Ground Task Force Warfighting Exercise at Marine Corps Air Ground Combat Center, Twentynine Palms, California.

MQ-9 REAPER
SPECIFICATIONS

Weight: 2,223kg (4,900lb)

Dimensions: L: 11m (36ft); Wingspan: 20.1m
(66ft); H: 3.8m (12.5ft)

Powerplant: Honeywell TPE331-10G-D
turboprop engine

Range:
1,850km (1,150mi)

Service ceiling:
15,240m (60,000ft)

Speed:
444km/h (240ktas, 276mph)

Weapons: AFG-114 Hellfire missiles; GBU-12
Paveway II; GBU-38 Joint Direct Munitions;
GBU-49 Enhanced Paveway II; GBU-54 Laser
Joint Direct Attack Munitions

TEST FLIGHT
An MQ-9 Reaper flies on a training mission over the Nevada Test and Training Ranger, 2019. The Reaper is armed with two AGM-114 Hellfire missiles which enable it to carry out precision strikes against ground targets.

a wide array of weaponry, including the GBU-12 Paveway II laser-guided bomb, AGM-14 Hellfire II air-to-ground missiles, the AIM-9 Sidewinder or the GBU-38 Joint Direct Attack Munition (JDAM). The mission kits and weapons loads can be adapted to particular operational requirements. The Reaper is controlled by a flight crew that includes a qualified pilot in the US Air Force, a sensor operator and a mission intelligence co-ordinator.

Requirements for special operations

US Air Force Special Operations Command requested that Reapers for special operations use should be capable of being packed ready for transport in less than eight hours to be flown anywhere in the world onboard a C-17 Globemaster III. Once unpacked, it should be ready for special operations missions with no support infrastructure.An extended range (ER) version of the Reaper has a wider wingspan with a wing spoiler, a four-blade propeller, heavy duty landing gear and external fuel tanks along with an improved fuel-management system.

The MQ-9A Reaper is deployed by various US Air Force squadrons in Air Combat Command. It is also deployed by US Air Force Special Operations Command. The Reaper is operated in various configurations by countries as diverse as France, Spain, Italy, Netherlands and the United Kingdom.

As the security environment has evolved, with the rapid proliferation of drones across the world and emerging threats from peer-group powers such as Russia and China, upgrades have been made to the MQ-9 Reaper to equip it to withstand growing competition. The upgrades include improved sensors and proofing against command-and-control jamming. A new open architecture design enables the Reaper to integrate new payloads to meet emerging threats. The upgraded version will also carry a wider selection of weapons. A counter-measures pod has been fitted to protect the Reaper from surface-to-air missile attacks.

RQ-7 Shadow

The RQ-7 Shadow is a tactical unarmed aircraft system (TUAS) that is capable of fulfilling several requirements at brigade combat team (BCT) level. These include reconnaissance and surveillance as well as target acquisition and force protection. The Shadow is compatible with a variety of radar and ground control systems.

RQ-7 SHADOW

An Unmanned Aerial Vehicle Operator with the 1st Engineer Battalion, 1st Infantry Division, operates an RQ-7 Shadow UAV during a surveillance training mission on an airfield at Camp Trzebien, Poland, 2019.

RQ-7B SHADOW

Country of origin:
United States
Manufacturer:
AAI Corporation
Operators:
US Army; US Special Operations
Command; US Marine Corps
First flight:
1991

The Shadow was developed
to fulfil a US Army requirement
for a battlefield unarmed aerial
system and was introduced
in 2002. It has a conventional
straight monoplane design with
fixed wings and an inverted
V-tail on the end of two tubular
booms. It has a pusher propeller
placed at the back of the
main fuselage. Underneath
the fuselage there is a gimbal-
mounted electro-optical and

RQ-7B SHADOW

A US Marine Corps RQ-7B Shadow aerial
vehicle of Marine Unmanned Aerial
Vehicle Squadron 3 launched from a
catapult at Camp Leatherneck, Helmand
Province, Afghanistan, 2011.

infrared camera with real-time
relay. The camera can be
digitally stabilized. A revised
version of the Shadow known as
the RQ-7B has a modified wing
and is longer than the original
version. It also has greater
endurance due to more effective
use of fuel. An improved fuel-
injected engine with dual spark
plugs was fitted in response to
engine problems experienced
in Iraq, relating to high levels of
heat and dust. The new wings
also include hardpoints from
which munitions can be carried.
The Shadow system consists
of four air vehicles, two universal

RQ-7B SHADOW SPECIFICATIONS

Weight:
75kg (165lb)
Dimensions:
L: 3.41m (11ft 2in); Wingspan: 3.4m (20ft)
Powerplant:
Rotary piston engine
Range:
735km (457mi)
Service ceiling:
4650m (14,983ft)
Speed:
207km/h (129mph)
Weapons:
N/A

ground control systems (UGCS) delivered on high-mobility multipurpose wheeled vehicles (HMMWVs), four One System remote video transceivers, one hydraulic launcher, two ground data terminals, as well as various associated trucks, trailers and support equipment. The equipment is managed by a Shadow platoon that includes 12 air vehicle operators, four electronic warfare repair personnel and three engine mechanics.

Apart from relaying information back to the brigade combat team, Shadows can also be used in conjunction with manned aircraft such as the AH-64 Apache to provide forward scouting, minimizing the danger to the manned aircraft.

Shadow systems were used extensively in both Iraq and Afghanistan and in March 2019 the US Army put out a request for a replacement of the RQ-7B Shadow.

MQ-1 Predator

The MQ-1 Predator is one of the most significant remotely piloted aircraft, and it has been proven in several conflict zones throughout the world. First developed in the 1990s for persistent aerial reconnaissance and forward observation, the Predator was soon armed and played a significant role in surgical strikes against high-value targets. Not only was the Predator successful in itself, but it was also the foundation for newer generation armed unmanned aerial vehicles such as Gray Eagle and the Reaper.

The Predator has a raised bulbous area at the front, straight wings extending from the fuselage and an inverted

PREDATOR MQ-1B

Country of origin:
United States
Manufacturer:
General Atomics
Operators:
US Air Force Special Operations Command
First flight:
1994

stabilizing fin and tail fins that point downwards at roughly 45° angles on both sides at the rear. A Rotax engine powers a pusher propeller also at the rear.

MQ-1 PREDATOR

An MQ-1 Predator of 163rd Reconnaissance Wing flying over the Southern California Logistics Airport, January 2012. The Predator is a game-changing reconnaissance and strike UCAV.

There are hardpoints on both main wings to carry munitions. The retractable undercarriage includes a nose wheel and two wheels on extended struts under the wings. The Predator carries a multi-spectral targeting system integrating an infrared sensor, colour/monochrome daylight TV camera, an image-intensified TV camera, a laser designator and laser illuminator.

The Predator was designed as a system that included four aircraft equipped with sensors and weaponry, a ground control station, a primary satellite link and spare equipment. The

Predator can be disassembled and loaded into a container that can be transported to its mission location. The ground control station can also be carried in a C-130 Hercules aircraft.

The concept of remote split operations meant that a small team could travel with the Predator system to the area of operations to make necessary arrangements for take-off, landing and maintenance whereas command and control of the mission itself could be taken over by a team in mainland United States once the aircraft was airborne. The

PREDATOR MQ-1B SPECIFICATIONS

Weight:
312kg (1130lb)

Dimensions:
L: 8.22m (27ft); H 2.1m (7ft); Wingspan: 6.8m (55ft)

Powerplant:
Rotax 91-4F 4-cylinder engine

Range:
1,239km (770 mi, 6.75nmi)

Service ceiling:
4,620m (25,000ft)

Speed:
135km/h (84mph, 70kts)

Weapons:
AGM 114 Hellfire missiles

Predator was operated by 11th and 15th Reconnaissance Squadrons and it has been deployed in a variety of conflict zones, including Bosnia, Afghanistan, Pakistan, Iraq, Syria, Iran, Somalia, Philippines and Libya. Predators were involved in strikes against al-Qaeda fighters and a Predator was also employed to take out a bunker occupied by al-Qaeda fighters on 4 March 2002 during the Battle of Takur Ghar, when US Army Rangers were pinned down by fire after their helicopter had been hit and crashed. In 2014, Predators were sent to Iraq to counter fighters of the Islamic State of Iraq and the Levant.

The Predator MQ-1 was in many ways a pioneering UAV. Lessons learned from crashes and other mission feedback led to improvements such as a de-icing system, longer wings and a more robust engine with turbo-power and fuel injection. The revised version was designated MQ-1B. The Predator was widely used by US Air Force Special Operations Command. The 3rd Special Operations Squadron was the largest Predator squadron in the US Air Force. Predator proved the value of a medium-sized long-endurance UAV with the option of carrying munitions for precision targeting. The advances made by the Predator

MQ-1B PREDATOR

A Dedicated Crew Chief prepares an MQ-1B Predator for a training mission, May 2013. This US Air Force Predator is armed with MGM-14 Hellfire air-to-ground missiles.

would then be consolidated and further developed in successor drones such as Gray Eagle and the Reaper.

Predator XP

The Predator XP is a revised version of the original Predator UAS that incorporates state-of-the-art technologies and is also licensed by the US Government for sale to a wider customer base, including the Middle East, North Africa and

The Flight of the Predator

The evolution of the RQ-1 Predator into the armed MQ-1 version was one of the most significant events in the development of armed combat aerial vehicles. Even before the attack on the United States on 11 September 2001, the RQ-1 Predator had been deployed to Afghanistan to hunt down Osama bin Laden. In an operation called Afghan Eyes, which was sanctioned at the highest level by both the US Department of Defense (DoD) and the Central Intelligence Agency (CIA), RQ-1 Predators were flown over Afghanistan from 7 September 2000. US military and CIA commanders were amazed by the quality of the footage gathered by the Predators. This included imagery of a tall man in a robe answering to the description of bin Laden. Their minds soon took the logical step that if they could see what appeared to be individuals such as Osama bin Laden what if the Predator UAVs were armed so that they could carry out a strike.

By February 2001, the Predators had been armed with AGM-114C Hellfire missiles for trials. The armed Predator received the designation MQ-1 in recognition of its new status and by June of that year, an MQ-1 Predator fired Hellfire missiles at a mock-up of bin Laden's Tarnak compound, proving that such a strike would be successful. Predator flights continued into September but by then the clock was ticking down. The events of that month would change the world forever, but it also marked a new dawn in aerial warfare.

ARMED RECON

The primary mission of the MQ-1 Predator is interdiction and conducting armed reconnaissance against critical, perishable targets. When the MQ-1 is not actively pursuing its primary mission, it provides reconnaissance, surveillance and target acquisition in support of the Joint Forces commander.

PREDATOR XP
Recognized for its operational readiness, the Predator XP features state-of-the-art technologies that augment its considerable abilities.

South America. The XP is fitted with automatic take-off and landing (ATOL), options for multiple sensors and line-of-sight (LOS) and beyond-line-of-sight (BLOS) data link systems for over-the-horizon operations. It also has a ground moving target indicator (GMTI) for locating moving vehicles. The XP is equipped for both land and maritime operations and its maritime suite includes maritime wide area search (MWAS) as well as an automatic identification system (AIS) for identifying ships at sea.

Predator C Avenger

This jet-powered unmanned combat aerial vehicle (UCAV) is designed for long-endurance missions at medium-to-high altitudes, including wide-area surveillance and strike missions over both land and sea. The manufacturers claim that it has much higher operational and flight speeds than the Predator B series of aircraft and that this enables quicker response and rapid positioning. However, after testing, the US Air Force concluded that the gains were not sufficiently different from the Predator B to warrant a significant order of

PREDATOR C AVENGER SPECIFICATIONS

Weight:
MTOW 8,255kg (18,000lb)

Dimensions:
L: 13m (44ft); Wingspan: 20m (66ft)

Powerplant:
Pratt & Whitney PW54B turbofan

Range/Endurance:
20 hours

Service ceiling:
15,240m (30,000ft)

Speed:
740km/h (400ktas, 460mph)

Weapons:
Hellfire missiles;
GBU-12/49, GBU-31
GBU-32, GBU-38 JDAM
GBU-39, GBU-16/48

**PREDATOR C
AVENGER**

Country of origin:

United States

Manufacturer:

General Atomics

Operators:

N/A

First flight:

2009/2016 (ER)

EURODRONE

Country of origin:
Germany, Spain, France and Italy

Manufacturer:
Airbus Germany; Airbus Spain; Dassault Aviation; Leonardo; Avio Aero

Operators:
Germany, Spain, France and Italy

First flight:
2026

EURODRONE SPECIFICATIONS

Weight:
MTOW 11,000kg (24, 251lb)

Dimensions:
L: 16m (162ft 6in); Wingspan: 30m (98ft 5in)

Powerplant:
2 Avio Aero Catalyst turboprops

Range/Endurance:
18–40 hours

Service ceiling:
13,700m (44,900ft)

Speed:
500km/h (310mph)

Weapons:
Precision-guided weapons

EURODRONE
A Eurodrone on display at the ILA International Aerospace Exhibition, Brandenburg, June 2022.

the UCAV. The Predator C has several hardpoints as well as an internal weapons bay that can carry precision munitions or additional sensors. The Predator C can use long-range sensors to remain in a stand-off position outside the range of enemy surface-to-air missile systems. The Avenger ER (Extended Range) was launched in 2016 to enhance the reach of the UCAV.

Eurodrone (European Medium Altitude Long Endurance Remotely Piloted Aircraft System (MALE RPAS))
The Eurodrone project was first launched in 2015 to produce a UAS for long-endurance intelligence, surveillance, reconnaissance and ground

support with precision-guided weapons. The aim was to produce an aircraft and systems that were entirely European. Development of the project is assigned to Airbus Germany, Dassault Aviation of France, Leonardo of Italy and Airbus Spain. A full-scale mock-up of the Eurodrone was shown at the Berlin Air Show in 2018. The aircraft has a sleek appearance with a raised area at the front, which gives it the appearance of a conventional manned aircraft, with wings positioned in the middle of the fuselage, a tail fin and two horizontal tailplanes supporting the two turboprop engines. The engines have pusher-type propellers facing the rear.

The Eurodrone has a modular design with multi-mission capabilities, including intelligence, surveillance and reconnaissance (ISR) missions along with targeting and weapons. The Eurodrone is produced as a system that includes three aircraft and two ground stations. The aim is to have one aircraft airborne, one prepared for take-off and another undergoing maintenance.

Each of the contributing nations has been assigned parts of the aircraft, its avionics and communications systems. Airbus Germany, the lead contractor, is responsible for the flight management systems, airspace integration systems as well as the landing gear and ground control stations. Airbus Spain is responsible for the fuselage and the flight control systems, engine fuel systems and tactical communications. Dassault Aviation is responsible for flight and landing systems. Leonardo will produce the wings and airborne mission systems. The Eurodrone will have five stations to support weapons, extra fuel tanks and

FALCO EVO

A Falco Evo on display at the 2017 Dubai Air Show. The front of the UCAV is uncovered to reveal the satellite communications (SATCOM) system.

other equipment required for the mission. The engines are to be supplied by Avio Aero of Italy, which is owned by General Electric.

Falco Evo

The Leonardo Falco Evo is a larger version of the original Falco UAV that was sold to countries such as Pakistan. Like its predecessor, the Falco Evo is primarily designed for military surveillance, although it can also be used for a broad range of homeland security missions.

The Falco Evo is a high-endurance UAV that can provide persistent surveillance for tactical use and can operate in all weather. With its multi-

spectral surveillance capabilities, it can provide stand-off, real-time target direction while operating over either land or maritime environments.

The Evo is delivered as a system that includes a ground control station (GCS), ground data terminal (GDT), ground support equipment (GSE) and three air vehicles fitted with equipment tailored to customer requirements.

The on-board equipment carried by the Evo includes electro-optical (EO)/infrared (IR) laser rangefinder (LRF)/laser designator, synthetic aperture radar (SAR), passive and active electric warfare (EW) equipment, satellite communications (SATCOM) and hyperspectral

PATROLLER

Country of origin:
France
Manufacturer:
Sagem
Operators:
French armed forces
First flight:
2009

sensor and communications intelligence (COMINT). Optional equipment includes Leonardo new-generation sensors such as the Gabbiano 20 multi-mode surveillance radar, P120SAR active electronically scanned array (AESA), Osprey multi-mode AESA radar as well as third-party sensor suites requested by operators. The Evo has both assisted and automatic flight management, automatic take-off and landing and automated area surveillance. This enables the aircraft to fly a pre-planned route while allowing the controller to intervene

manually if necessary. The Evo can also be used to pass live data to small frontline units.

Patroller MALE

The Patroller remote-controlled, medium-altitude, long-endurance (MALE) unmanned aerial vehicle (UAV) was designed and manufactured by Sagem in association with Stemme for the French armed forces. Its first flight took place in Finland in 2009 and it was displayed at the Paris Air Show in the same year. The Patroller is based on the Stemme S-15 motor glider and has a robust airframe with the engine at the front powering the nose propeller. The wings are placed high and include hardpoints for extra loads, including armaments. It has a traditional T-shaped tail on the end of a slender dragonfly rear fuselage section. The propeller is powered by a Rotax engine and the aircraft is equipped with a retractable tricycle

PATROLLER MALE UAV SPECIFICATIONS

Weight:
750kg (1653lb)
Dimensions:
L: 8.52m (28ft); Wingspan: 18m (59.1ft); H 2.45m (8ft)
Powerplant:
Rotax 114 F2 engine
Range/Endurance:
4,000km (2,485mi)
Service ceiling:
6,000m (20,000ft)
Speed:
199km/h (124mph)
Weapons:
AGM-114 Hellfire missiles; laser-guided rockets

PATROLLER

A logo sits on the fuselage of a Patroller UAV, manufactured by Safran SA, on the second day of the Paris Air Show in Paris, June 2013.

undercarriage. The Patroller is produced in three variants, depending on its intended role. The Patroller-R is primarily designed for intelligence, surveillance, target acquisition, reconnaissance and battle damage assessment. The two wing hardpoints are used for additional fuel tanks. The Patroller-S is designed primarily for airborne surveillance. This might include border and coastal surveillance, search and rescue (SAR) and law enforcement. It is equipped with an airborne surveillance radar. The Patroller-M is designed for maritime operations and is used by the French Navy. It carries maritime patrol radar.

The Patroller has a low radar, heat and sonic signature and a quiet engine. The aircraft is fitted with an automatic take-off and landing system that allow the UAS to return safely to base in the event of any breakdown in communication with the ground control system (GCS).

The Patroller is equipped with a global positioning system (GPS), inertial navigation system (INS), a high-resolution, colour electro-optic camera, triplex avionics and a laser telemetry system. It is also fitted with Eurofit 410 electro-optic (EO) and infrared (IR) sensors. It carries an identification friend or foe (IFF) transponder and laser designator. The synthetic

aperture radar (SAR) can provide digital terrain elevation data (DTED). The Patroller can carry Lockheed Martin AGM-114 Hellfire air-to-surface missiles or laser-guided rockets.

Bayraktar TB2

The Bayraktar TB2 is a medium-altitude long-endurance (MALE) unmanned combat aerial vehicle (UCAV). Capable of both intelligence, surveillance and reconnaissance (ISR) as well as armed attack missions, the TB2 proved to be one of the most significant and successful UAVs of its type. The TB2 has a blended aerodynamic shape with straight wings and an

inverted V-tailplane design. The petrol engine is positioned at the rear of the fuselage and drives a two-blade variable pitch pusher propeller. There is a gyro-stabilized gimbal under the fuselage housing the optical equipment. Two hardpoints under each wing can carry four laser-guided smart munitions. The TB2 has a modular design and the wings and tailplanes can be dismantled as units. The fuselage and wings are mostly constructed from a carbon fibre composite.

The TB2 system consists of six aerial vehicles, two ground control stations (GCS), three ground data terminals (GDT), two remote video terminals (RVT) and ground support equipment. A mobile ground control station can be deployed to forward areas mounted on a truck. Consistent with NATO ACE III shelter standards, the shelter has air conditioning and nuclear, biological and chemical (NBC) protection.

The TB2 has been used operationally in Turkish internal conflicts, in Libya, Syria, Nagorno-Karabakh and in Ukraine. The TB2 had a significant impact on all of these conflicts, including the destruction of tanks, multiple launch rocket systems, surface-to-air missile batteries and other assets. An improved version,

BAYRAKTAR TB2

Country of origin:
Turkey
Manufacturer:
Baykar
Operators:
Turkey; Ukraine; Azerbaijan; Pakistan
First flight:
2014

BAYRAKTAR TB2 SPECIFICATIONS
Weight:
MTOW 650kg (1433lb)
Dimensions:
L: 8.5m (27ft 10in);
Wingspan: 12m (39ft 4in)
Powerplant:
105hp petrol engine
Range/Endurance:
27 hours
Service ceiling:
5,400–7,600m (18–25,000ft)
Speed:
220–130km/h (70–120 knots)
Weapons:
4 laser-guided smart munitions

SOKIL-300

The heavy long-range attack UAV
SOKIL-300 at the international exhibition
Arms and Security, 2021.

the TB2S, is fitted with a satellite communications system to reduce the likelihood of enemy jamming.

Sokil-300

The Sokil-300 is an unmanned combat aerial vehicle (UCAV) capable of both intelligence, surveillance and reconnaissance (ISR) as well as combat missions. It has straight wings and canted tailplanes on the top of the fuselage as well as a fin below the fuselage. The engine is located at the rear, driving a pusher propeller. There is a gimbal under the nose that carries cameras and sensors. Four hardpoints under the

wings can carry guided missiles.

Horlytsia

The Horlytsia is the first unmanned combat aerial vehicle (UCAV) to be produced in Ukraine and it is designed to supplement the fleet of #TB2 Bayraktar UAVs operated by Ukraine. The Horlytsia is capable of visual electro-optical aerial reconnaissance, communications support, target location, ground moving target positioning and tracking as well as direct combat attack. The Horlytsia system consists of four UAVs, a ground control station and transportation equipment and spares. The

Snake Strike

Ukrainian Bayraktar TB2 UCAVs scored significant successes against Russian tanks, armoured vehicles and self-propelled guns during the early months of the war. They were also used effectively by the Ukrainian navy in strikes against Russian naval assets in the Black Sea and near the port of Odessa, as well as Snake Island at the mouth of the Danube river. The Ukrainian navy operates a more advanced version of the Bayraktar TB2 than the Ukrainian Air Force. It is recognizable visually by its three-blade propeller and it also carries a more advanced infrared camera for night operations as well as a GPS-ONSS anti-jamming aerial. The TB2 is armed with either a NAM-C ultra-lightweight, laser-guided glide bomb or the larger and more powerful NAM-L.

In operations around Snake Island, the Bayraktar TB2 carried out several successful strikes against Russian assets. On 2 May 2022, Ukrainian naval TB2s attacked and destroyed two Russian Raptor assault boats. On 6 May, TB2s destroyed a Russian SA-15 air defence system on the island, making it possible for Ukrainian air force SU-27 Flanker fighters to attack Russian positions on the island. Later, Russian forces attempted to bring in a replacement SA-15 system on a supply boat and a TB2 destroyed the system as it was being unloaded. On 8 May, Russian forces attempted to land reinforcements by helicopter and a TB2 destroyed the Mi-8 HIP helicopter as it was unloading troops. Two more Russian assault boats were also hit by TB2 strikes during this period. The destruction of the air defence system by the TB2s compounded the problem of trying to locate and hit the small, low-flying TB2s with classic radar defences.

COMBAT TEST
Bayraktar TB2 UAVs seen during test flights at the military base in Hmelnitski, Ukraine, March 2019.

design is a cylindrical fuselage with a high-mounted straight wing. Twin booms reach backwards and are joined by two inwardly canted tail fins. The engine is positioned at the rear of the fuselage. The UAV has a fixed tricycle undercarriage. The UAV is equipped with electro-optical (EO) infrared (IR) sensors with automatic tracking and aiming. It has one hardpoint under each wing to carry munitions.

AN-BK-1 HORLYTSIA

The AN-BK-1 Horlytsia ('Turtle Dove') unmanned aerial vehicle (UAV) was developed by the Antonov State Enterprise for the Ukrainian Armed Forces in Kyiv, Ukraine.

Orion-E/Orion Inokhodets

The Orion is a medium-altitude long-endurance (MALE) unmanned aerial vehicle (UAV) that has been produced in a mainly reconnaissance and export version (Orion-E) as well as an armed combat version for Russian military use (Orion Inokhodets). The design of the Orion is similar to that of the US Predator. It has a slim fuselage with straight wings and canted tailplanes. The engine is at the rear and drives a pusher propeller. The armed version carries two hardpoints under each wing to carry munitions or guided missiles. It has a non-retractable tricycle undercarriage. The Orion is capable of signal intelligence (SIGINT) and communications intelligence (COMINT). It is also capable of laser-designation of targets and has a ground moving target indicator (GMTI).

KRONSTADT ORION-E
Russian unmanned aerial vehicle developed by Kronstad` AFK Sistema at the International Aviation and Space Salon, MAKS 2019.

ORION-E/ORION INOKHODETS SPECIFICATIONS

Weight:
MTOW 1,150kg (2,335lb)

Dimensions:
L: 8m (26ft 2in); Wingspan: 16m (52ft 5in)

Powerplant:
N/A

Range/Endurance:
250km (160mi) / 24 hours

Service ceiling:
7,500km/h (4660 miles)

Speed:
120km/h (75mph)

Weapons:
Laser-guided anti-tank missiles

ORION-E/ORION INOKHODETS

Country of origin:
Russia

Manufacturer:
Kronstadt Group

Operators:
Russian armed forces

First flight:
2016

The Orion has the ability to direct and position ground radars. In 2019, the Orion had combat testing during operations in Syria. In 2020, Orion UAVs were delivered to the Russian armed forces.

Altius

The Altius is a medium-altitude, long-endurance unmanned combat aerial vehicle (MALE/UCAV) designed for reconnaissance, armed strike and electronic warfare missions. It is deployed by the Russian air force and navy. The Altius is a relatively large UAV and is powered by two turboprops, one on each wing. The tailplanes are canted. It can carry air-dropped or air-launched ordnance, including precision-guided munitions (PGMs), missiles and bombs.

Bayraktar Akıncı

This Akinci is an unmanned combat aerial vehicle capable of providing intelligence, surveillance and reconnaissance (ISR) as well as carrying out combat missions. It is also capable of supporting manned fighter jets in their operations. It is equipped with dual satellite communication systems and air-to-air radar. It also has electronic support systems, collision avoidance radar and synthetic aperture

BAYRAKTAR AKINCI

Country of origin:
Turkey
Manufacturer:
Baykar
Operators:
Turkish armed forces
First flight:
2019

radar. It can carry a variety of electronic payloads including simultaneous electro-optic/ infrared/laser designation (EO/ IR/LD), multi-mode active electronically scanned array (IESA) radar and signals intelligence. It uses advanced AI features to collect and process data from on-board sensors and cameras. The Akinci is fitted with four hardpoints to carry laser-guided smart munitions such as NAM-T, NAM-C and NAM-L. It can also carry long-range stand-off weapons. The ground control station is capable of both line-of-sight (LOS) and beyond-line-of-sight (BLOS) satellite communications.

BAYRAKTAR AKINCI
The Akinci Unmanned UCAV was manufactured by the Turkish technology company Baykar.

TAI Aksungur

Based on technology from the TAI Anka series of UAVs, the Aksungur is the largest medium-altitude long-endurance (MALE) UAV produced by TAI. The Aksungur is an adaptable UAV platform that can be modified for different missions, including intelligence, surveillance and reconnaissance (ISR), signals intelligence (SIGINT), maritime patrol and attack. The Aksungur can maintain an ISR or signals intelligence mission for about 24 hours and a maritime patrol or attack mission for about three hours.

The design of the Aksungur includes high-mounted wings.

BAYRAKTAR AKINCI SPECIFICATIONS

Weight:
MTOW 6,000kg (2,335lb)
Dimensions:
N/A
Powerplant:
N/A
Range/Endurance:
7,500km (4,00mi) / 24 hours
Service ceiling:
13,700m (45,000ft)
Speed:
N/A
Weapons:
Smart munitions and missiles

AKSUNGUR

Country of origin:
Turkey
Manufacturer:
Turkish Aerospace Industries
Operators:
Turkish navy
First flight:
2019

Under each wing there is a turboprop engine with a three-bladed propeller. The engine nacelles extend into booms that support the tailplane structure at the back, with vertical stabilizers and a horizontal tailplane across the top of them. The tricycle landing gear can be retracted in flight to increase aerodynamic efficiency. Under each wing there are three hardpoints that can carry either munitions or equipment such as sonar buoys for maritime patrols. There is a gimbal with 360° traverse mounted under the nose. On-board payloads include electro-optical (EO), infrared (IR), laser designator (LD), laser rangefinder (LRF), cameras, synthetic aperture radar (SAR), ground moving target indicator, inverse synthetic aperture radar (GMTI-ISAR) sensors and a variety of air-to-ground weapons. The maritime payload also includes an automatic identification

TAI AKSUNGUR

The Anka is a medium-range unmanned combat aerial vehicle which has a highly adaptable modular design. It is produced in three versions, each of which has a different mission focus.

AKSUNGUR SPECIFICATIONS

Weight:
1,800kg (3,968lb)
Dimensions:
L: 12m (39ft 4in); Wingspan: 24m (78ft 9in)
Powerplant:
4-cylinder turbocharged piston engine
Range/Endurance:
6,500km (4,000mi) / 60 hours
Service ceiling:
12,192m (40,000ft)
Speed:
250km/h (160mph)
Weapons:
Guided missiles; rockets; small bombs

system, a sonobuoy pod and a MAD boom. Communications payloads include satellite communications (SATCOM), a personnel locating system (PLS), VUHF radio relay and an airborne communications mode pod. The Aksungur is capable of fully autonomous operations and it has an automatic return home and emergency landing mode if communications with the ground control station are lost.

TAI Anka

The TAI Anka is a medium-altitude, long-endurance unmanned aerial vehicle and it has been produced in three main versions. The Anka-A is designed primarily for intelligence, surveillance and reconnaissance (ISR). The Anka-B features a synthetic

aperture radar and a friend or foe identification (FFI) system. The Anka-S is equipped with ASELSAN CATS (common aperture targeting system), a FLIR system, a flight computer and satellite communications (SATCOM). It can also carry four Roketsan NAM-L laser-guided munitions.

The TAI Anka has a similar profile to the Predator and Reaper UAVs. It has a tubular fuselage with an aerodynamically bulged nose. It has high-mounted straight wings and a pair of outward canted tail fins on either side of the rear engine housing. The engine drives a pusher propeller. There is an optics gimbal under the nose. The tricycle undercarriage is retractable.

Typical payloads for any of the Anka models include an

TIA ANKA

The Anka drone, 8.6 metres long and with a wingspan of 17.6 metres, is manufactured in Turkish Aerospace's huge, ultra-secure facilities in Ankara, which cover four million square metres of hangars. 10,000 people, including 3,000 engineers, were employed here in 2021.

electro-optic, colour day camera (EO day TV), electro-optic, forward-looking, infra-red/laser rangefinder/laser designator and spotter camera (EO/FLIR/LRF/LDS), synthetic aperture radar/ground moving target indicator (SAR/GMTI) and inverse synthetic aperture radar (ISAR). The Anka is delivered as a system that includes three air vehicles, a ground control station (GCS), a ground data terminal (GDT), an automatic take-off and landing system (ATOLS), a transportable image exploitation system (TIES), a remote video terminal (RVT) and ground support equipment. The Anka can fly a pre-programmed mission and can also perform automatic take-off and landing.

Denel Dynamics Seeker-400

The Seeker-400 is a development of the proven Seeker II unmanned aerial system. It is 30 per cent longer than the Seeker II and carries more advanced equipment. Designed primarily for intelligence, surveillance and reconnaissance (ISTAR), it has hardpoints under the wings that can be used to carry weapons or spare fuel tanks. The Seeker-400 can operate day or night and in extreme weather. It can be configured for either manual or autonomous flight or equipment control.

The Seeker-400 can operate at a direct-line-of-sight range of up to 250km (155mi), providing real-time reconnaissance, target location and designation, artillery fire support as well as electronic intelligence (ELINT) and electronic support measures (ESM). On-board equipment may include a colour daylight camera with a zoom lens; a laser range finder; a laser designator; infrared thermal imager; a day colour or monochrome spotter camera

SEEKER-400
The latest version of the Seeker is capable of reconnaissance, target location and electronic intelligence (ELINT) as well as precision strikes.

or a night spotter camera. It is fitted with automatic take-off and landing.

The Seeker-400 is delivered as a system that may include four to six UAVs, a mission control unit (MCU) and tracking and communications unit (TCU); mission-specific equipment; field support equipment; and optional secondary MCU and TCU. The system can be transported in two C-130 aircraft.

Yabhon United 40

The Yabhon United 40 is a medium-altitude long-endurance (MALE) unmanned aerial vehicle (UAV). It is designed to carry out intelligence gathering, reconnaissance and communications relay. It is capable of supporting a variety of operations including special forces missions. The Yabhon 40 can carry munitions of various types and it can designate targets. The UAV has an S-type shape and a twin-wing configuration. The bulbous nose tapers to a large vertical stabilizer at the rear. A three-blade propeller is located at the rear. The munitions carried in the underwing pods may include air-to-ground missiles or dumb or guided bombs. A naval version of the Yabhon 40 can deploy sonobuoys and carry a single lightweight torpedo. Apart from the United Arab Emirates itself, the Yabhon 40 is also operated by Russia, Egypt and Algeria.

Cloud Shadow

The Cloud Shadow is a high-altitude long-endurance (HALE) unmanned aerial vehicle and is produced in three main versions. The CS-1 has an emphasis on imagery reconnaissance, the CS-2 on electronic reconnaissance and the CS-3 on reconnaissance and armed strike. The Cloud Shadow has an aerodynamic bulbous nose and swept-back wings. The tailplanes are canted and there is an air scoop at the rear that feeds the turbojet engine. The standard equipment for most versions includes an electro-optical/

ADCOM SYSTEMS UNITED 40
This United 40 UCAV is designed for naval operations. The navalized version can deploy sonobuoys for anti-submarine warfare and can also carry a torpedo for air-to-sea strike.

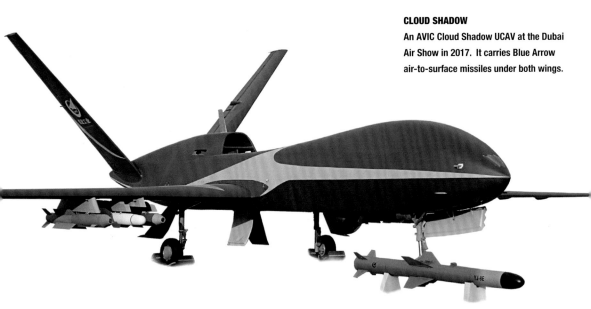

CLOUD SHADOW
An AVIC Cloud Shadow UCAV at the Dubai Air Show in 2017. It carries Blue Arrow air-to-surface missiles under both wings.

CLOUD SHADOW SPECIFICATIONS

Weight:
2,300kg (5071lb)

Dimensions:
L: 9m (29ft 6in); Wingspan: 20m (65ft 7in)

Powerplant:
Turbojet

Range/Endurance:
90km (180mi)

Service ceiling:
15,000m (49,000ft)

Speed:
620km/h (385mph)

Weapons:
Missiles; guided bombs

CLOUD SHADOW

Country of origin:
China

Manufacturer:
Aviation Industry Corporation of China (AVIC)

Operators:
China

First flight: 2016

infrared/EOIR payload pod for aerial surveillance, intelligence gathering, observation, target selection and reconnaissance. The package includes high-resolution imaging sensors. Two hardpoints are located under each wing for carrying smart munitions or missiles. The Cloud Shadow can be flown in either autonomous or remote-control modes. Mission commands are

sent from the ground control station (GCS) to the UAV via a data link. The Cloud Shadow is delivered as a system that includes three UAVs, one ground control station (GCS) and strike payloads where relevant.

CH-5 Cloud Rainbow

The CH-5 Cloud Rainbow is a medium-altitude long-endurance (MALE) unmanned aerial vehicle (UAV) and, as its designation suggests, the fifth of the Rainbow series of UAVs. The CH-5 is capable of carrying out a range of military missions, including intelligence, surveillance, targeting and reconnaissance as well as patrol and strike missions. Similar in appearance to the RQ-9 Reaper, the CH-5 Rainbow has straight wings and two canted tailplanes. The engine and propeller are mounted on the rear. The newest version of the CH-5 features a turbocharged heavy-fuel engine for longer endurance. The CH-5 has three hardpoints under each wing for carrying munitions.

CH-7 Rainbow

The CH-7 Rainbow is a flying-wing style, stealth unmanned aerial vehicle that is designed to carry out advanced reconnaissance support and armed strike missions. The CH-7 is capable of strategic information detection, continued reconnaissance and air defence suppression as well as combat support.

The CH-7 has been designed in such a way as to minimize enemy radar detection and this extends not only to the flying-wing shape, but also to details such as paint coatings. Munitions are carried within a concealed bomb bay so as to maximize aerodynamic efficiency.

The CH-7 Rainbow is capable of operations against enemy airborne early warning and control (AEWAC)

CH-5 CLOUD RAINBOW
A CH-5 Cloud Rainbow UCAV at the China International Aviation and Aerospace Exhibition in Zuhai, 2016. It carries AR-1 or AR-2 compact supersonic anti-tank missiles.

CH-5 RAINBOW SPECIFICATIONS

Weight:
2,225kg (4,905lb)

Dimensions:
L: 11.2m (36ft 8in); Wingspan: 21m (68ft 10in)

Powerplant:
Turboprop

Range/Endurance:
10,600km (6214mi)

Service ceiling:
9,000m (29,500ft)

Speed:
220km/h (137mph)

Weapons:
Missiles; smart weapons

TB-001

A Sichuan Tengden's TB-001, nicknamed 'Twin-tailed Scorpion' by the People's Liberation Army Air Force (PLAAF), flies at the 13th China International Aviation and Aerospace Exhibition in Zhuhai, southern China, 28 September 2021.

TENGOEN TB-001 SPECIFICATIONS

Weight:

2,000kg (4,409lb)

Dimensions:

L: 10m (32ft 10in); Wingspan: 20m (65ft 7in)

Powerplant:

two turboprops

Range/Endurance:

6,000km (3,700mi) / 35 hours

Service ceiling:

8,000m (26,000ft)

Speed:

250km/h (155mph)

Weapons:

Air-to-surface missiles; laser-guided bombs

TENGOEN TB-001

Country of origin:

China

Manufacturer:

Sichuan Tengden

Operators:

China

First flight:

2017

platforms. The CH-7 can also be deployed on anti-ship missions.

This medium-altitude long-endurance (MLE)

unmanned aerial vehicle (UAV) is designed for both reconnaissance and armed combat missions. The UAV has a twin-tail design with two booms extending from under each wing where they are joined by a horizontal tailplane. There is a turboprop engine under each wing driving a three-blade propeller. The UAV is capable of satellite communications and it can also carry Blue Arrow air-to-ground missiles. It is fitted with a retractable bicycle undercarriage. There is also a version of the TB-001 that has a third engine at the rear of the fuselage driving a pusher propeller.

Tengoen TB-001 Twin-tailed Scorpion

This medium-altitude long-endurance (MLE) unmanned aerial vehicle (UAV) is designed for both reconnaissance and armed combat missions. The UAV has a twin-tail design with two booms extending from under each wing where they are joined by a horizontal tailplane. There is a turboprop engine under each wing driving a three-blade propeller. The UAV is capable of satellite communications and it can also carry Blue Arrow air-to-ground missiles. It is fitted with a retractable bicycle undercarriage. There is also a version of the TB-001 that has a third engine at the rear of

the fuselage driving a pusher propeller.

WZ-7 Soaring Dragon

This unmanned combat aerial vehicle is designed for high-altitude, long-endurance missions and is similar in appearance and role to the Northrop-Grumman RQ-4 Global Hawk. It is fitted with a turbo-jet engine with the air intake mounted on the top of the fuselage in front of the tail. Apart from its reconnaissance and surveillance role, the WZ-7 is also capable of carrying munitions for strike missions.

WZ-7

A WZ-7 Soaring Dragon high-altitude reconnaissance UCAV at its first official unveiling at the 13th China International Aviation and Aerospace Exhibition, September 2021.

WZ-7 SOARING DRAGON SPECIFICATIONS

Weight:
2,000kg (4,409lb)
Dimensions:
L: 14.33m (47ft); Wingspan: 24.86m (81ft 4in)
Powerplant:
Guizhou WP-13 turbojet
Range/Endurance:
2,000km (1,200mi)
Service ceiling:
18,000m (59,000ft)
Speed:
1000km/h (621mph)
Weapons:
Laser-guided bombs; air-to-surface missiles

VERTICAL TAKE-OFF & LANDING (VTOL) UAVs

The advantages of vertical take-off and landing (VTOL) are obvious. VTOL aircraft can take off from and land on or in confined spaces such as areas with no runways or a naval ship deck. However, relatively large manned helicopters can also be easily exposed to ground fire while hovering, even from relatively straightforward hand-held weapons such as a rocket-propelled grenade (RPG). Due to their size, manned helicopters are also more likely to be picked up by enemy radar. Smaller in size than a conventional manned helicopter, a VTOL UAV is less likely to be picked up by conventional enemy radar. With semi-autonomous or fully autonomous features, VTOL UAVs can also incorporate learning technologies that expand their operational performance and capabilities.

Another advantage of unmanned VTOL aerial vehicles is that they can operate in cooperation with manned conventional helicopters to enhance operational efficiency and reach, enabling the manned helicopter to operate in stand-off mode while the UAV advances into contested air space or high-risk areas, thus minimizing the risk to the crew. Naval versions of unmanned VTOL aerial vehicles now incorporate technology that enables them to take off and land from moving ship decks in adverse weather conditions, reducing the likelihood of error by the operator.

AIRBUS VSR 700

The VSR 700 is designed to be deployed from frigates, destroyers and other naval ships to supplement manned helicopters in roles such as anti-submarine warfare (ASW).

Hybrid VTOLs

Vertical take-off and landing aircraft have both advantages and limitations. They cannot fly at the speed of a fixed-wing aircraft and do not have

"Hybrid UAVs are particularly useful for small units operating covertly, such as special forces, where the ability of the UAV to take off and land vertically reduces their potential exposure to hostile forces."

the same range or the ability to minimize fuel expenditure through gliding ability. They also require higher levels of maintenance. Fixed-wing aircraft, on the other hand, depending on their size, require either a runway or some form of initial propulsion such as a catapult. The advances

in hybrid technology have harnessed the advantages of both types of aircraft to create an unmanned aerial vehicle that can lift vertically from confined spaces and then transition into conventional forward flight. There are a variety of designs, as described in this chapter, some of which incorporate small rotors on extensions for vertical lift and a main rotor for forward flight. Hybrid UAVs are particularly useful for small units operating covertly, such as special forces, where the ability of the UAV to take off and land vertically reduces their potential exposure to hostile forces, whether in a forest or an urban environment.

MQ-8B/MQ-8C Fire Scout

The MQ-8B and MQ-8C Fire Scout unmanned autonomous

NAVAL SUPPORT DRONE
An MQ-8B Fire Scout during an exercise to check automated deck landing on USS *Nashville*.

helicopters were tested by both the US Army and the US Navy. The two systems are differentiated by the air vehicle design. The MQ-8B is based on the Schweizer 333 manned helicopter whereas the MQ-8C is based on the commercial Bell 407 helicopter. The MQ-8B Schweizer airframe is powered by a Rolls-Royce Model 250 C20W engine.

The US Army and US Navy took turns blowing hot and

MQ-8B FIRE SCOUT

Country of origin:
United States
Manufacturer:
Northrop-Grumman
Operators:
United States Navy
First flight:
2006

MQ-8B FIRE SCOUT
The MQ-8B is the smaller version of the Fire Scout which is deployed on US Navy Littoral Combat Ships (LCS). It can operate alongside manned helicopters in maritime operations.

cold over the systems. Initially the US Navy lost interest in the MQ-8B whereas the Army's interest increased. In due course, the Army came to the conclusion that the RQ-7 Shadow served its needs better and the Navy then revived its interest in the MQ-8B.

The Navy fitted a multi-mission maritime radar in the MQ-8B and has also tested weapons capability that includes advanced precision kill weapon system (APKWS). The MQ-8B system tested for the Army included a laser rangefinder and designator that enabled the Fire Scout to

MQ-8B FIRE SCOUT SPECIFICATIONS

Weight:
940.3kg (2,073lb)
Dimensions:
L: 9.6m (31.5ft); H: 2.9m (9ft 8in)
Powerplant:
Rolls-Royce 250 420hp
Range/Endurance:
40 minutes
Service ceiling:
3,810m (12,500ft)
Speed:
157km/h (85 knots, 97.8mph)
Weapons:
Advanced Precision Kill Weapon System (APKWS)

detect, locate, identify, track down and designate targets quickly and accurately, as well as carrying out battle damage assessments.

Following its renewed interest in the Fire Scout programme and its first successful landing of an unmanned helicopter on a US Navy ship in 2006, the US Navy deployed the Fire Scout on Littoral Combat Ships in order to exploit its sensor package for submarine, mind and surface warfare. MQ-8Bs were also deployed to Afghanistan to carry out intelligence, surveillance and reconnaissance (ISR) and to Libya for Operation United Protector in which a Fire Scout was shot down by pro-Gaddafi forces while on a reconnaissance mission. In many ways, this demonstrated the value of the unmanned system as no lives were lost. Two MQ-8Bs were lost to

accidents. One in Afghanistan and one while returning to land on its mother ship at sea. Analysis revealed that one of the crashes was due to a fault in the navigational system and the other was also a software failure. More stringent checks were introduced to obviate such faults.

The advantage of the next-generation MQ-8C is that the airframe is larger and is capable of providing extended endurance, with over 10 hours on station, a range of 241km (150mi) and a greater payload capacity. The MQ-8C has the ability to take off and land on any suitable ship as well as on unprotected landing sites.

The sensor suite on the MQ-8C includes a FLIR Systems AN/AAQ-22D BITE Star II electro-optical/infrared and laser range-finding target designation turret as well as a Leonardo AN12PY-8 Osprey 30 active electronically scanned

MQ-8C FIRE SCOUT

This MQ-8C Fire Scout is based on the Bell 407 helicopter airframe. It can take off and land autonomously from aviation-capable ships and from unprepared onshore landing zones.

array radar. This gives the Fire Scout long-range, all-weather detection, tracking and radar imaging capabilities. The benefits include situational awareness, over-the-horizon targeting and ISR.

RQ-16 T-Hawk

This vertical take-off and landing (VTOL) ducted-fan, small unmanned air vehicle was developed by Honeywell in a project launched by the Defense Advanced Research Projects Agency (DARPA), which was then transferred to the US Army Future Combat System (FCS) programme. The twin piston engines of the T-Hawk provide enough lift for the UAV to reach altitudes of up to 3048m (10,000ft) and speeds of up to 128km/h (80mph), but in operational use the T-Hawk was mostly used in a localized 'hover and stare' mode to provide imagery of objects and areas of interest to its controllers. This might include a roadside bomb or navigation through confined spaces, whether in an urban or countryside environment.

In 2007, the US Navy ordered 20 of the UAVs to be deployed to Iraq by the US Multi-Service Explosive Ordnance Disposal Group. The aim was to minimize risk to personnel when inspecting unexploded devices. The following year the US Navy ordered another 272 T-Hawks

DESERT PATROL
A British soldier watches as a Tarantula Hawk Micro Remote Piloted Air System (RPAS) hovers over the desert in Afghanistan.

RQ-16 T-HAWK SPECIFICATIONS

Name:
16 T-Hawk
Weight:
4.5kg (10lb)
Dimensions:
W: 59.6cm (23.5in);
H: 46cm (18in)
Powerplant:
56cc Boxer twin piston engine
Service ceiling:
3,200m (10,500ft)
Speed:
130km/h (81mph)
Weapons:
N/A

RQ-16 T-HAWK
Country of origin:
United States
Manufacturer:
Honeywell
Operators:
US Army; US Navy; British Army
First flight:
2008

Sonobuoy

One of the tasks of the new vertical take-off and landing (VTOL) unmanned aerial systems (UASs) that are being deployed in increasing numbers to world navies is the use of sonobuoys for submarine detection. A sonobuoy is typically dropped from an aircraft or dangled or trailed in the water. A canister is dropped, usually with a small parachute to slow the descent and the system deploys once it hits the water. A hydrophone sensor then descends beneath the surface while a communication device remains floating on the surface to relay signals to an aircraft.

An active sonobuoy will send out sound energy signals and wait for them to bounce back from a solid object such as a submarine hull. A passive sonobuoy will wait for sounds emanating from a submarine engine or any other acoustic signals. The advantages of distributing sonobuoys from a VTOL UAV are that they are usually smaller than manned helicopters and therefore less likely to be picked up by enemy radar and they can free up manned helicopters for other missions. They also reduce risk to crew when entering contested areas.

PREPARATION
Aviation Ordnanceman 1st Class Anthony Petito, locks a sonobuoy into the chute. Petito is assigned to Patrol Squadron 62 (VP-62), located at Naval Air Station Jacksonville, Florida.

RECOVERY MISSION
Sailors assigned to the 'Raptors' of Helicopter Maritime Strike Squadron (HSM) 71, recover a sonobuoy using an MH-60R Seahawk helicopter.

for their Explosive Ordnance Disposal (EOD) teams. The US Army also ordered the T-Hawk UAVs for reconnaissance, surveillance, target acquisition (RSTA) and laser designation, using its unique hover utility to provide essential information in terrain where the vision of the small unit was limited. Although the intention had been to supply the T-Hawk to brigade combat teams (BCTs), the US Army changed its mind and cancelled the order. Instead, they placed an order for the RQ-20 Puma. One of the reasons for the retirement of the T-Hawk was the high noise levels of its engines, which could place both the UAV and its controllers at risk. However, for missions such as convoy overwatch and route clearance, the noise of vehicles was likely to mask the noise of the UAV. The T-Hawk was ordered by the UK Ministry of Defence and deployed by British Army counter-IED teams in Afghanistan from 2010.

Snipe Nano Quadromotor UAS

Capable of close-range intelligence, surveillance and reconnaissance (ISR) missions, the Snipe UAS is a quadromotor portable system that is designed to provide operators with the information they need to make tactical decisions in their immediate environment. Carried in a belt

SNIPE NANO

The highly portable Snipe Nano can be quickly deployed by a single soldier to provide an instant view over a wall or round a corner in contested urban or field operations.

SNIPE NANO QUADROMOTOR UAS

Country of origin:
United States
Manufacturer:
AeroVironment
Operators:
US Army
First flight:
2017

SNIPE NANO QUADROMOTOR UAS SPECIFICATIONS

Weight:
140g (4.9oz)
Dimensions:
N/A
Powerplant:
4 battery-powered motors
Range:
1km (0.6mi)
Service ceiling:
N/A
Speed:
35km/h (21.7mph)
Weapons:
N/A

pack by an individual operator, the Snipe UAS has an almost identical mission profile to the Black Hornet UAS.

The Snipe has four electric motors that drive four rotor blades. There are powered by replaceable batteries. It has enough power to fly for over 30 minutes. The air vehicle is controlled from a ruggedized tablet that operates a Windows 7 OS. The UAS can either be controlled manually or programmed for waypoint navigation using a global positioning system (GPS). It can fly at speeds of up to 55km/h (22mph) and has a very low noise signature. The EO/IR cameras in the Snipe

provide real-time video and the UHF radio enables excellent communications beyond line of sight. The cameras and sensors are located in a tilt system at the front of the UAS to provide optimum viewing angles.

VSR 700 Vertical Take-off and Landing (VTOL) Unmanned Aerial System (UAS)

The VSR 700 is a multi-mission, vertical take-off, naval unmanned aerial vehicle (UAV) that is based on the manned Calvi G2 light helicopter. Still under development by Airbus in 2022 as part of the Systeme de drone aérien de la Marine (SDAM) programme, the project

has had a contract with the French Navy since 2017. The VSR 700 is designed to operate from existing Mistral assault frigates, destroyers and future frigates, including the FD1 and FREMM.

The mission profile for the VSR 700 includes intelligence, surveillance, target acquisition and reconnaissance (ISTAR). It is also capable of anti-submarine warfare (ASW) through a module designed by Thales. The UAS also carries

VSR 700

The VSR 700 can land autonomously either on ship decks or on land. It is capable of persistent surveillance operations.

VSR 700 SPECIFICATIONS

Weight:
760kg (1,675lb)
Dimensions:
L: 6.2m (19.6ft); H: 2.28m (7.4ft);
Rotor blades: 7.2m (23.5ft)
Powerplant:
Diesel or jet powered diesel engine
Range:
10 hours max
Service ceiling:
6,000m (20,000 ft)
Speed:
185km/h (120 knots, 115mph)
Weapons:
N/A

AWHERO

An AWHero tactical rotary unmanned aerial vehicle (RUAV). The AWHero can perform a wide spectrum of maritime and battlefield missions.

AWHero is backed by a fine pedigree and features the same safety standards that are found in a conventional manned helicopter. This includes systems redundancy and high reliability levels as well as triple redundant flight control and navigation systems.

The nose bay of the AWHero houses an electro-optical and infrared (EO/IR) turret to identify, locate and track land sea targets. It can also transmit high-definition video and images. The range of equipment options includes synthetic aperture radar (SAR), automatic identification system (AIS), electronic support measures (ESM), identification friend or foe (IFF), electronic support measures (ESM) and maritime radar. The manufacturers claim that the RYAS fitted with Gabbiano TS20 ultra-light radar provides four times greater area coverage than a UAS of the same weight category equipped with optical sensors.

The compact design of the AWHero means that it can be easily stored in naval ship hangars and it can also operate in confined spaces. As part of their strategic alliance, Leonardo and

high-performance day/night cameras and maritime radar. The VSR 700 can also be deployed for search and rescue (SAR), carrying a deployable raft for survivors.

The VSR 700 is designed to cover a broad area, raising its mother ship's horizon to identify emerging threats. Due to its compact size and sleek design, the VSR 700 can be carried onboard alongside conventional manned naval helicopters and it can also operate alongside them to provide reconnaissance and targeting information to the manned aircraft.

Systems carried by the VSR 700 include communication and intelligence (COMINT), electro-optics and infrared (EO/IR) sensors and an automatic identification system (AIS). It is also equipped with Airbus DeckFinder, enabling easier take-off and landing on moving ships' decks.

Optional uses for the VSR 700 include fishery protection, action against smugglers and other forms of coastal surveillance. With its ability to remain on station for up to 10 hours and its low profile, it presents formidable opportunities to commanders and intelligence analysts.

AWHero Rotary Unarmed Air System

Designed for both maritime and land operations, the AWHero RUAS is a highly versatile platform for intelligence, surveillance, reconnaissance (ISR) and data collection as well as anti-submarine warfare and combat support. The RUAS can also provide mine countermeasures, riot control, force protection and beyond-line-of-sight (BLOS) communications relay.

Built by a company with a solid reputation for reliability in helicopter manufacture, the

SKELDAR V-200
SPECIFICATIONS

Weight:
MTOW 40kg (88lb)

Dimensions:
L: 4m (13ft); W: 1.2m (3ft 11in)

Powerplant:
Hirth heavy fuel parallel twin two-stroke engine

Range:
6+ hours

Service ceiling:
3,000m (9,842ft))

Speed:
140km/h (75 knots, 86mph)

Weapons:
N/A

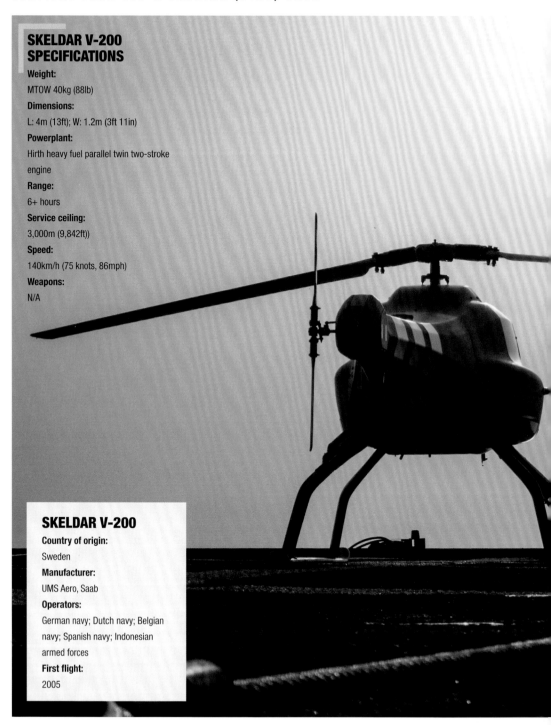

SKELDAR V-200

Country of origin:
Sweden

Manufacturer:
UMS Aero, Saab

Operators:
German navy; Dutch navy; Belgian navy; Spanish navy; Indonesian armed forces

First flight:
2005

SKELDAR V-200
The Skeldar is a highly adaptable VTOL UAV that is capable of surveillance, electronic warfare, border protection and anti-submarine warfare (ASW).

Northrop-Grumman offered the AWHero system to the Royal Australian Navy.

Skeldar V-200

The Skeldar V-200 is a medium-range, vertical take-off and landing (VTOL) unmanned aerial vehicle (UAV). The Skeldar is designed primarily for surveillance, 3D mapping, intelligence gathering, electronic warfare and light cargo transportation. It is capable of autonomous take-off and landing and its two-stroke heavy-fuel engine can operate on Jet A-1, JP-5 and JP-8 fuels. The modular payload may include laser pointers, laser rangefinders, electro-optical and infrared (EO/IR), 3D mapping and signals intelligence (SIGINT).

The UAV control station can be integrated into a military ground vehicle or the combat management system in a ship. The Skeldar can be used on either land or sea operations and can land easily on variable terrain on land or on the deck of a ship. It has already been selected by the German navy for use on their K130 Braunschweig class corvettes. It has also been ordered by both the Royal

Netherlands Navy and Belgian navy for use on mine counter-measures vessels. The Skeldar is also deployed by the Royal Canadian Navy, Spanish navy and by Indonesian armed forces.

Ziyan Blowfish

The Blowfish is a vertical take-off and landing (VTOL) unmanned aerial vehicle (UAV) designed for all-weather reconnaissance and supply tasks. The Blowfish has a main rotor, tail rotor and four-point skid undercarriage. It has an optics sensor under the nose and it can be fitted with a variety of sensors according to mission requirements. Sensors include electro-optical (EO) and infrared (IR) cameras and

LIDAR scanners. For maritime operations, it can be fitted with an automatic ship identification transceiver. The Blowfish supports long-range HD video links and 4G communications modules for real-time image transmission. The Blowfish is capable of distributed intelligence technology to fly in swarm formation with other drones with automated avoidance. Apart from its reconnaissance tasks, the Blowfish can also carry light loads such as medical supplies.

FVR-90 Airframe

The FVR-90 Airframe is a vertical take-off and landing (VTOL) unmanned aerial system (UAS) with hybrid quadrotor

technology. This allows the air vehicle to rise vertically from the ground or a ship's deck before transitioning to forward flight. This gives the UAS the flexibility and small footprint of a VTOL aircraft with the speed and range of a conventional fixed-wing aircraft. The main engine is located at the rear of the fuselage and powers a pusher propeller.

The FVR-90 is fitted with a modular nose and two wing hardpoints that present a number of options for carrying mission-related equipment. This may include the WESCAM MX-8 stabilized multi-sensor, multi-spectral imaging system; the electro-optical (EO) and infrared (IR) system and a mid-wave infrared (MWIR) camera. It can also carry a laser rangefinder and a laser illuminator. Electronic equipment is mounted on a four-axis gimbal.

The FVR-90 can be controlled with a small mobile ground control station either on a Windows laptop or a laptop fitted with Datalink.

Merlin UAV V-BAT

The V-BAT is a vertical take-off and landing (VTOL) unmanned aerial system (UAS) with

BLOWFISH A3

A Blowfish A3 combat swarm system VTOL UAV at the UMEX exhibition in Abu Dhabi. The Blowfish A3 is capable of carrying a wide range of munitions.

MERLIN UAV V-BAT SPECIFICATIONS

Weight:
56.6kg (125lb)

Dimensions:
L: 2.7m (9ft); Wingspan: 2.9m (9ft 6in)

Powerplant:
Suter TAA288 engine

Range/Endurance:
10 hours

Service ceiling:
6,096m (20,000ft)

Speed:
90km/h (56mph)

Weapons:
N/A

directed fan technology. It is designed for runway and equipment-independent launch and recovery, and it can easily be transported to and from its launch site in a truck and assembled in under 20 minutes. The V-BAT can take off and land in high winds and it can also be operated at sea on crowded flight decks, taking advantage of its small footprint. The V-BAT is launched vertically rather than horizontally. Once aloft, the V-BAT can be programmed to operate autonomously.

The V-BAT is designed to support a variety of mission-appropriate equipment and sensors, including EO/MWIR camera, AIS and land/maritime wide-area search (WAS) technologies. The system is controlled via an artificial intelligence software programme called Hivemind.

JUMP 20

Country of origin:
United States
Manufacturer:
AeroVironment
Operators:
United States Special Operations
Command
First flight: N/A

This system enables the
V-BAT to adapt to changing
conditions and threats and
independently choose the most
appropriate options.

The V-BAT was under
consideration by the US Army
for its Future Tactical UAS
(FTUAS) system to replace

the RQ-7 Shadow. It was also
trialled by the US Marine Corps
and a naval version was also
under development.

AeroVironment Jump 20

The Jump 20 is a medium
unmanned aerial vehicle
(UAV) that has the ability to
transition from vertical take-
off and landing (VTOL) to
forward flight on fixed wings.
This means that it does not
require a runway or any form of
launch or recovery device. The
ingenious design incorporates
four electric motors positioned
on booms that extend forward
and backward from each wing.
These drive small propellers
for vertical lift. At the front of

the fuselage, there is a petrol-
powered engine driving a
nose propeller for horizontal
flight. Once the Jump is aloft,
it transitions from vertical to
forward modes, with the wings
providing the necessary uplift
as it flies to its target area of
operations.

The Jump system is
designed to be straightforward
to operate and it can be
unpacked, set up and ready

JUMP 20

A soldier assigned to 1st Engineer
Battalion, 1st Infantry Division, conducts
an engine start on the JUMP 20 prior to
a launch during the FTUAS capabilities
assessment at Fort Riley, Kansas,
April 2020.

for flight in under an hour. Once on its mission, the Jump can provide multi-sensor intelligence, surveillance and reconnaissance (ISR). The Jump 20 is designed to carry modular and easily customizable equipment packages that are adapted to mission requirements. Standard equipment includes a TASE gyro-stabilized gimballed electro-optical infrared (E/IR) imaging system; EO/IR cameras to provide video data and target tracking in real-time day and night; LiDAR synthetic aperture radar (SAR); communications relay; 3D mapping sensors; communications intelligence (COMINT); signals intelligence (SIGINT); and standard navigational lights. Real-time

sensor data is transmitted to the operators via a data link (L, S or C band). A Piccolo autopilot provides fully autonomous flight using a flight control processor and on-board sensors.

The Jump 20 was selected by United States Special Operations Command (USSOCOM) as part of the Indefinite Delivery, Indefinite Quantity (IDIQ) mid-endurance unmanned aircraft systems (MEUAS) programme. The Jump 20's unique qualities enable it to provide enhanced multi-sensor ISR services for special operations teams in a variety of tactical scenarios. The system was also under consideration by the Royal Australian Navy (RAN) for its tactical unmanned aircraft

AEROSONDE HQ
The Aerosonde HQ is a runway-independent UAV that uses Hybrid Quadrotor technology to achieve vertical take -ff and landing (VTOL).

programme. The Jump 20's VTOL abilities make it highly suitable for operations from naval vessels. The Jump 20 was also a contender for the US Army's Future Tactical Unmanned Aircraft System (FUAS) programme.

Textron Aerosonde HQ

The Aerosonde HQ small unmanned aircraft system (SUAS) employs hybrid quadrotor technology for runway-independent vertical take-off and landing (VTOL). This means that the UAS can be deployed without the use of

any other auxiliary equipment apart from its control station. A crew of four can unpack and launch the system in under 20 minutes.

With its low visual and auditory signatures, the Aerosonde HQ can be used for covert operations as well as expeditionary or sea operations. It has a wide array of equipment options that include synthetic aperture radar (SAR); signals intelligence (SIGINT); communications intelligence (COMINT); 3D mapping; full-motion video (FMV) with day or night imaging and voice communications relay.

The air vehicle can be programmed to operate autonomously with little more than a push of a button by the operator. The UAS then transitions from vertical to horizontal flight and proceeds on its mission. The UAS is fitted with four quadrotors on

booms extending forwards and backwards from each wing whereas forward thrust is provided by a Lycoming heavy fuel engine driving a pusher propeller at the rear of the fuselage.

ThunderB

The ThunderB is a vertical take-off and landing (VTOL) small, tactical, long-range, long-endurance fixed-wing unmanned aerial vehicle (UAV). The vertical rotors are positioned on extensions under each wing, giving the ThunderB the advantages of both VTOL and conventional forward flight, including speed and range. The ThunderB carries a variety of sensors that enable it to provide intelligence, surveillance, target acquisition and reconnaissance (ISTAR) as well as communications. The payload includes an infrared (IR) camera, a day camera and a laser pointer. It

TROJAN
The Trojan hybrid VTOL UAV provides the operators with the tactical advantages of aboth vertical take-off and landing and the range and speed of fixed-wing flight.

can also carry gyro-stabilized photogrammetric equipment for high-resolution mapping imagery. The ThunderB features automatic take-off and landing and it can operate in adverse weather. It is accompanied by a rapidly deployable, easily portable and intuitive ground control system. The ThunderB has a low acoustic, visual, thermal and radar signature that makes it ideal for use by special forces.

Trojan

The Trojan is a vertical take-off and landing (VTOL) unmanned aerial vehicle (UAV) that is also capable of conventional fixed-wing flight. It has four sets of vertical rotors located on booms that extend from

Trendsetter

The delivery of large numbers of WanderB and ThunderB hybrid VTOL UAVs to an unnamed European armed force was more than just a record-breaking multimillion pound deal; it was the sign of a trend towards small and medium portable UAVs of this type. Some of the new UAVs were purchased for use by special forces, which underlined the operational importance of hybrid VTOL UAVs. The WanderB and ThunderB systems enable operational flexibility and provide real-time intelligence and situational awareness for special forces and other infantry operators. They can provide intelligence, surveillance, target acquisition and reconnaissance capabilities to enable special forces to keep abreast of the evolving modern battlefield. Man-packable and quickly deployable, the WanderB and ThunderB hybrid VTOL UAVs can be quickly deployed for either day or night operations.

the fuselage as well as a main pusher propeller at the rear for forward flight. The Trojan is capable of intelligence, surveillance and reconnaissance (ISR) as well as wide-area persistent surveillance (WAPS). It has an optics suite at the front of the fuselage and the Trojan uses multiple sensors. It is capable of interpolating

intelligence information onboard for more rapid communication to the forces that need it most. The Trojan communicates with the ground control station (GCS) either via a radio link or through satellite communications (SATCOM). The ground control station can be controlled by a single operator and is capable of handling up to four UAVs. The adaptability and agility of the Trojan make it highly suitable for special forces missions.

People's Drone 1 VTOL

This crowdfunded small vertical take-off and landing (VTOL) unmanned aerial system (UAS) provides Ukrainian forces with an eye in the sky at the frontline. It carries an electro-optical/infrared payload including a day camera and thermal imaging camera. It can be flown in either pilot-assisted or autonomous modes. The PD-1 VTOL achieves vertical lift through four rotors on extensions under the wings.

PEOPLE'S DRONE-1 VTOL SPECIFICATIONS

Weight:
MTOW 40kg (88lb)

Dimensions:
L: 2.54m (8ft 2in); Wingspan: 4m (13ft 1in)

Powerplant:
61cc 2-cylinder 4-stroke engine

Range/Endurance:
100 km/h (62mph) / 10 hours

Service ceiling:
3,000m (9,843ft)

Speed:
140km/h (87mph, 76 knots)

Weapons:
N/A

UAVs & UCAVs IN DEVELOPMENT

The exponential increase in the number and capabilities of UAVs in the first quarter of the 21st century signalled a transformation of aerial warfare. Although UAVs would continue to carry out essential intelligence, surveillance and reconnaissance (ISR) missions – as well as targeted strikes for both strategic commanders and frontline units or special forces – the prospects had expanded to forms of aerial warfare previously only seen in the realms of science fiction. UAVs could now fly at hypersonic speeds and were capable of delivering fatal blows to strategic assets such as aircraft carriers. The concept of the loyal wingman was being rapidly developed whereby a manned fighter aircraft could entrust attack and defence to a semi-autonomous drone flying alongside. The loyal wingman drone could be a force multiplier and widen the reach of the manned aircraft through its on-board sensors and weapons systems. The flying missile rail concept envisaged a manned aircraft handling a flock of unmanned combat aerial vehicles (UCAVs), each of which was capable of firing intelligent munitions.

Perhaps the most revolutionary concept hinged on the extent to which UCAVs could operate autonomously, effectively making their own decisions about which targets to attack. The current common arrangement for UCAVs such as the MQ-9 Reaper is for the operator to set the target and for the UCAV to carry out the attack semi-autonomously or with human guidance.

XQ-58A VALKYRIE

An XQ-58A Valkyrie low-cost unmanned aerial vehicle launches at the US Army Yuma Proving Ground, Arizona, December 2020.

A more advanced version is for the operator to merely supervise an operation that the UCAV carries out autonomously.

> **"The force-multiplying effect of drones becomes more important as they can fill the numbers gap at relatively low cost."**

The development of advanced UCAVs of this type follows a parallel logic to the development of manned fighter aircraft. As new-generation manned fighters become ever more technologically advanced and sophisticated, so do they become more expensive and even major powers tend to buy fewer of them. In this scenario, the force-multiplying effect of drones becomes more important as they can fill the numbers gap at a relatively lower cost. Drones are less expensive to build than manned aircraft, partly because they do not require all the safety systems that would be required to protect a human pilot.

MQ-Next

The MQ-9 Reaper has been one of the most iconic and renowned unmanned combat aerial vehicles (UCAV). The nemesis of jihadist insurgents and ISIL fighters, it has carried out surgical strikes against ground targets for years. Although the MQ-9 Reaper has received upgrades to proof it against a more intensive developing combat scenario in contested non-permissive environments, inevitably questions are being asked in the US Air Force about what system should replace it. Several big players in the US defence industry have responded to the US Air Force request for information, including General Atomics, the manufacturer of the MQ-9 Reaper, Lockheed Martin, Northrop-Grumman, Boeing and Kratos. General Atomics has produced a stealthy, jet-powered concept design.

Lockheed Martin has offered a stealthy flying-wing design that will be adapted to US Air Force requirements, whereas Northrop-Grumman's flying-wing design is similar to the X-47B for the US Navy. Designs from Boeing and Kratos were still in the pipeline at the time of writing. Factors under consideration included adaptability, survivability and affordability. Contractors also mulled over the possibility of a multiple systems approach with a high-end system as well as multiple smaller and

CONTROL MODULE
An airman from Canon Air Force Base sits at the control module of MQ-9 Reaper at Hurlburt Field, Florida, in 2014. Next-generation multirole unmanned combat aerial vehicles will play an increasingly significant role in aerial operations.

V-247 VIGILANT

Country of origin:
United States
Manufacturer:
Bell Helicopter
Operators:
N/A
First flight:
2019

expendable systems. The new drone is likely to incorporate increased autonomy, artificial intelligence and machine learning. The system is likely to be capable of air-to-air operations and the ability to intercept ballistic missile launches or shoot down incoming cruise missiles.

Bell Vigilant V-247 tilt-rotor UAV

The V-247 will combine the vertical lift capability of a helicopter with the speed and range of a conventional fixed-wing aircraft. It is designed to provide persistent surveillance as well as combat capability. Due to its vertical lift capability, it can operate from naval vessels as well as confined areas on land. It is capable of electronic warfare, intelligence, surveillance and reconnaissance (ISR), as well as command, control, communications and computers (C4) with plug-and-play mission packages.

The open architecture modular payload enables

V-247 VIGILANT SPECIFICATIONS

Weight:
7,257kg (15,990lb)
Dimensions:
Wingspan: 20m (65ft)
Powerplant:
N/A
Range/Endurance:
2,500nmi
Service ceiling:
7620m (25,000ft)
Speed:
555km/h (300 knots, 345mph)
Weapons:
MK-50 torpedo, Hellfire or JAGM missiles

XQ-58 VALKYRIE

Country of origin:
United States
Manufacturer:
Kratos Defense and Security
Solutions
Operators:
United States Air Force
First flight:
2019

XQ-58 VALKYRIE SPECIFICATIONS

Weight:
1,134kg (2,500lb)
Dimensions:
L: 9.1m (30ft); Wingspan: 8.2m (27ft)
Powerplant:
Turbojet/turbofan
Range/Endurance:
5,600km (3,500 miles)
Service ceiling:
14,000m (45,000ft)
Speed:
882kmh (548mph)
Weapons:
External and internal precision
guided bombs

the UCAV to be customized according to mission requirements. It can carry high-definition sensors, light detection and ranging (LIDAR) modules, sonobuoys and 360-° surface radar modules. It can be armed with MK-50 torpedoes or Hellfire or JAGM missiles.

XQ-58 Valkyrie

This stealthy unmanned combat aerial vehicle (UCAV) has been designed by Kratos in response to US Air Force Low Cost Attritable Strike Demonstrator (LCASD) programme. Its role would be to provide loyal wingman escort duties to F-22 or F-35 advanced fighter jets during combat missions, either individually or as part of a drone swarm. It will carry its own surveillance payloads and weapons systems and

will provide protection to the manned aircraft as necessary, including absorbing enemy fire and scouting into dangerous airspace. It has been designed to fly at high speed and over long ranges and will carry weaponry both in internal bomb bays and on wing hardpoints. Speeds will be around Mach 0.9 and it will be capable of operating at 15,240m (50,000ft). Kratos has worked with the US Air Force Skyborg programme to prove that an autonomous unmanned system flying in close cooperation with high-end manned fighter aircraft is now a reality.

MQ-28 Ghost Bat
A product of the Boeing Airpower Teaming System and created in collaboration with the Royal Australian Air Force (RAAF), this is a stealthy

XQ-58A VALKYRIE

The XQ-58A Valkyrie demonstrates the separation of the ALTIUS-600 small unmanned aircraft system in a test at the US Army Yuma Proving Ground test range, March 2021. The test was the first time the weapons bay doors had been opened in flight.

MQ-28 GHOST BAT

Developed by Boeing Australia, the MQ-28 Ghost Bat multirole unmanned combat aerial vehicle is designed as a teaming system that will operate alongside manned aircraft as a loyal wingman force multiplier.

multirole unmanned aerial vehicle that is conceived as a force multiplier aerial system. It will be capable of flying alongside manned aircraft, including the RAAF F-35A, F/A-18F, E-7A and KC-30A, to provide support and perform autonomous missions with the use of artificial intelligence. The modular characteristics of the MQ-28A Ghost Bat include the ability to swap the entire nose section according to mission requirements. This unmanned combat aerial system has been designed and produced in Australia and the Royal Australian Air Force have ordered six with an estimated production date of 2025.

Skydweller

This medium-altitude long-endurance (MALE) unmanned aerial vehicle (UAV) was developed from a manned Solar Impulse 2 aircraft. It is fitted with photovoltaic cells that gather solar energy during flight, giving the UAV unlimited endurance and range. Its intelligence, surveillance and reconnaissance (ISR)

payloads enable the Skydweller to provide wide-area and sustained surveillance.

Scaled Composites Model 437

The Model 437 is a loyal wingman project that was a candidate for either the US Air Force Skyborg project or the Royal Air Force Mosquito programme. Developed by Northrop-Grumman subsidiary Scaled Composites, the Model 437 is likely to reach Mach 0.6 and a ceiling of 7,600m (25,000ft).

BAE Magma

The BAE Magma unmanned aerial vehicle (UAV) is a technological development project devised by BAE Systems and the University of Manchester, which explores the advantages of using supersonically blown air to replace the conventional moving flight-control surfaces on an aircraft. One of the advantages of replacing the moving surfaces is that it enhances the stealth properties of the aircraft by

Mobile Force Protection

It is the nature of defence research that while resources are poured into technologies that can seek and destroy adversaries, it has to be simultaneously geared towards defence methods to protect friendly forces. The exponential rise in drone technologies has placed conventional forces, for example, in a routine convoy, at risk from attack by self-guided, small unmanned aerial systems (sUAS). These may suddenly appear in a swarm and overwhelm the conventional defences available on standard military vehicles such as the high-mobility, multipurpose wheeled vehicle (HMMWV). New systems would need to be devised to detect such attacks while they are still at sufficient range and to neutralize them before they can do harm. As with all drone technologies, those that inflict the sting must also develop the antidote.

TANK KILLER

A tank reportedly destroyed by a drone in North Wollo, Ethiopia, January 2022. Conflicts in Africa, the Middle East and Eastern Europe have demonstrated the increasing effectiveness of drone air-to-ground strikes.

smoothing over edges and gaps. The aerial vehicle is also lighter, more reliable, has fewer moving parts and is cheaper to operate. Control of the aircraft is generated through thrust vectoring. The Magma is a flying-wing arrowhead design that currently includes outward canted vertical tail fins, although these are likely to be removed in the fully developed version.

BAE Taranis

The Taranis is a development project for a UK unmanned combat aerial vehicle (UCAV) that will fly intercontinental missions and can carry out sustained surveillance, intelligence gathering, target designation and combat strike missions. The Taranis incorporates stealth technologies that maximize the ability to carry out missions undetected. These include a low-profile flying-wing design, special skin coating, minimal structural protrusions and a shielded engine exhaust. The Taranis is also capable of high levels of autonomy, making decisions in response to changing mission parameters. The Taranis is a collaborative project between BAE Systems, Rolls-Royce, GE Aviation Systems, QinetiQ as well as the Ministry of Defence. The BAE Systems subsidiary Integrated Systems Technologies is responsible for supplying computers, command and

TARANIS SPECIFICATIONS

Weight:
N/A
Dimensions:
L: 12.43m (40ft 9in); H: 4m (3ft 1in)
Powerplant:
Rolls-Royce Adour turbofan
Range/Endurance:
N/A
Service ceiling:
N/A
Speed:
Supersonic
Weapons:
Guided missiles

control, communications, intelligence, surveillance, target acquisition and reconnaissance (C4iSTAR). The Taranis features open-system architecture similar to that found in the Hawk trainer and Typhoon fighter. The image collection and exploitation (ICE) system developed by BAE Systems enables the autonomous collection and distribution of high-quality imagery. The Taranis also builds on previous BAE Systems UAV programmes including Kestrel, Raven, Corax and HERTI.

Dassault nEUROn

This experimental unmanned combat aerial vehicle (UCAV) has been developed by a consortium that includes

BAE TARANIS

Country of origin:
United Kingdom
Manufacturer:
BAE Systems
Operators:
N/A
First flight:
2013

Dassault Aviation as the lead along with involvement from aerospace interests in Greece, Italy, Spain, Sweden and Switzerland. It will be a stealthy, autonomous UCAV that can operate in medium-to high-threat combat zones.

The nEUROn has a delta-wing shape and is powered by a single Rolls-Royce/ Turbomeca Adour MK951 jet engine. It features a

TARANIS
The Taranis uses stealth technology to minimize its radar profile.

trapezoidal air intake and radar-reducing exhaust assembly. Weapons are carried internally in a weapons bay. The aerial system is similar in size to a conventional fighter such as the Rafale and is capable of speeds of up to Mach 0.8.

Baykar TB3

The Baykar TB3 is an enhanced and more powerful version of the Baykar TB2. It has greater capacity than the TB2 and it has folding wings for use in confined spaces such as a naval carrier deck. The TB3 will include up to six hardpoints for carrying

weaponry, including a wide array of precision-guided munitions. It is intended for use by the Turkish Navy on their projected new carrier the TCG Anadolu.

Baykar Kizilelina

The Baykar Kizelilina, part of the MIUS project, is an unmanned combat aerial vehicle (UCAV) designed to fly combat missions from the projected Turkish Navy TCG Anadolu carrier. The MIUS will be a fifth-generation fighter system designed to compete with similar concepts produced by other nations. The TCG Anadolu has been

BAYKAR KIZILELINA SPECIFICATIONS

Weight:
MTOW 6,000kg (12,228lb)
Dimensions:
L: 14.7m (48ft 3in); Wingspan: 10m (32ft 10in)
Powerplant:
Turbofan engine
Range/Endurance:
930km (467mph)
Service ceiling:
14,000m (45,000ft)
Speed:
735km/h (467mph)
Weapons:
Guided missiles or bombs

Loyal Wingman

The term 'loyal wingman' describes an airpower teaming system developed by Boeing and other aerospace companies whereby a manned aircraft is accompanied by teamed drones that are tied into the same mission parameters. The concept was part of the Skyborg project developed by the US Air Force Research Laboratory. The project follows from the logic that the rising costs of producing high-tech manned fighters first reduces their numbers and also increases the impact of their potential loss. By teaming semi-autonomous drones with manned fighters, military researchers plan to reduce costs while increasing the combat mass available to an air force. As they have a lower cost and do not have a human pilot, the loyal wingman drones have been described as 'attritable', which is to say that they can suffer damage or loss without creating massive financial or tactical impact. While the loyal wingman drones will remain under the control of the pilot or co-pilot of the 'mother' aircraft, they will also have enough autonomy and mission knowledge to carry out tasks independently, whether it is defending the manned fighter from attack, using their on-board sensors to provide information or scouting ahead to identify and if necessary destroy enemy radar or surface-to-air missile batteries, thus creating a clear corridor for the manned aircraft. Such has been the success of the Skyborg project that both large and small aerospace companies are now producing viable loyal wingman drones for advanced tests, opening the way for the teamed missions of the near future.

F-22 RAPTOR SUPPORT
An artist's concept of a Lockheed Martin F-22 Raptor accompanied by three Loyal Wingman drones.

designed as a platform for attack drones, including the Baykar TB3. The carrier could support up to 80 drones. The MIUS fighter will be highly adaptable, agile and capable of short take-off and landing. Projected speeds are Mach 0.8 and beyond and the UCAV will have an endurance of five hours. The MIUS will be armed with air-to-air missiles, cruise missiles or guided munitions, depending on operational requirements. The

first flight for the MIUS was scheduled for 2023. Larger weapons will be carried in internal bays while smaller munitions will be carried on underwing hardpoints. The design is tail-less but has two canted vertical stabilizers. It has air intakes on both sides of the fuselage. The MIUS will have artificial intelligence (AI) and intelligent fleet autonomy technology enabling it to either support manned aircraft in a loyal wingman configuration or fly independently.

Divine Eagle

Although full details are not available for this unmanned aerial vehicle (UAV), it is thought to be the largest UAV in the Chinese inventory and is comparable in size to the Global Hawk. A jet-powered, high-altitude long-endurance (HALE) UAV, the Divine Eagle has a twin-boom layout with a low-wing configuration. A single turbojet engine sits between the twin vertical fins on top of the horizontal mainplane at the rear. The bulbous nose section probably houses radomes and the sensor mission suite. Dorsal blisters on the fuselage may house SATCOM or other mission-related equipment. The Divine Eagle carries up to seven AESA radars. The UAV

DIVINE EAGLE

Country of origin:
China
Manufacturer:
Shenyang Aircraft Corporation
Operators:
Chinese armed forces
First flight:
2020

DIVINE EAGLE SPECIFICATIONS

Weight:
240kg (529lb)
Dimensions:
L: 4.7m (50ft); Wingspan: 10.5m (132ft)
Powerplant:
Turbojet engine
Range/Endurance:
3–5 hours
Service ceiling:
5:000m (16,404ft)
Speed:
150km/h (93mph)
Weapons:
Guided missiles and guided bombs

takes off and lands on a tricycle undercarriage. The Divine Eagle is likely to have been developed to support anti-ship missiles and thereby poses a significant threat to the naval vessels of the United States and its allies.

Picture Credits